Emotional Resilience

How to manage your mental and emotional states for optimal results in life!

CLAUDIA FERRYMAN

RAINMAKER BOOKS
www.rainmakerstrategies.org
First Edition, May 2019

ISBN: 9781099272455

Many thanks to all those who have encouraged me to write this book.

I dedicate it to all those who are seeking a life of greater joy and fulfillment!

Contents

INTRODUCTION

I felt compelled to write this book for over five years now. I was inspired by numerous conversations with family, friends, students and clients who expressed their feelings of anxiety and constant stress over such things as the uncertainty of future career prospects, technological changes, social media, cyberbullying, lack of money, scarcity of good jobs, workplace isolation, negative political instability, helping elderly parents and caring for children with health challenges while trying to take care of their own selves. A great majority expressed their worries about their retirement income, climate change, and the increase in global violence.

Humanity has advanced in so many ways, but our ability to effectively manage stress and emotional reactions to stressors continues to pose the greatest challenge. In the face of so much pressure, it is more important than ever to have the fortitude and inner strength to rise above our circumstances.

Both my life experiences and the work that I've done over the past twenty years have led me to the conclusion that building one's resilience is the most powerful way to navigate through a stressful life. The capacity to recover quickly from difficult situations can make all the difference between overcoming adversity and feeling helpless and out of control.

As a personal coach and certified facilitator, I have taught resiliency workshops for years and have witnessed people make profound breakthroughs; quite often I get notes or emails from clients who tell me that the tools and concepts they learned had a lasting and positive impact on their coping strategies.

After hearing the success stories of so many people who were positively impacted by their work with me, I decided that writing a book on emotional resilience is an integral part of bringing together proven research, tools and therapeutic methods to equip others with the ability to overcome stress and setbacks, and to live their best lives.

Viktor Frankl, an Austrian neurologist and psychiatrist who survived the Holocaust and became a symbol of resilience, had this to say about it: *"When we are no longer able to change a situation, we are challenged to change ourselves. Everything can be taken from a man but one thing: the last of the human freedoms—to choose one's attitude in any given set of circumstances, to choose one's own way. Between stimulus and response there is a space. In that space is our power to choose our response. In our response lies our growth and our freedom."*

These words have been an inspiration for me throughout my own journey toward resilience. Growing up as an racial minority and a female in Canada in the seventies posed many challenges. I found myself navigating through bullying, stereotypes and sexism, all which taught me to tap into my inner strength as a way to conquer adversity and cultivate my own resilience.

In grade 4, a friend and I had to plan an escape route from school every day in order to avoid a gang of six older students who were bullying younger kids. The group was made up of six boys and two girls. They primarily targeted ethnic students or girls to physically attack. Their gripe started with my friend, but because I defended her, I too became a target.

My friend and I would decide which stairwell to meet at after class. We would run as fast as possible from school, crossing the street and hiding behind a block of buildings, and from there we made our way home. We were in constant fear of being caught, and this went on for weeks. We'd heard that the bullies would kick and punch their victims, so how could we make them stop?

We started to brainstorm options other than just running, like skipping the last class or maybe telling a teacher or parent about what was going on. In the end, we decided against these ideas since we thought that telling adults might cause more problems.

One day, I decided that I was tired of running. I went to the principal and told her about the bullies and abuse other kids had suffered. As a result, two of the boys from that gang got expelled, and this caused the group to dissolve. Later that year, I was confronted by a couple of members of their group. They tried to hit me, and I pushed them away. After they realized that I was not afraid of them, they never bothered me or my friend again.

Although I constantly looked behind me on my walk home for months after, I reminded myself that I had the strength to stand up for myself and other students, and that my act of courage had made a difference.

To sum up, I learned the following about resilience:

- If you keep your goal and vision in mind, you can move beyond the intermediate obstacles

- If you rely on strong beliefs and values, you will see the advantage in being adaptable and agile in the face of adversity

- Don't dwell on what's going wrong – become solutions-oriented, take charge and take action

- You need to make the best of the tools you have at hand and work on a solution. There will always be people who have it easier, and people who have it harder than you. The key is to use the tools, experiences and unique gifts you possess to your strategic advantage.

- You can *reframe* the meaning in almost any negative experience. Even the worst times can provide learning experiences and produce an outcome that may be beneficial in the long run, one that strengthens your determination, forces you to evaluate what is truly important to you, and ultimately plants seeds of resilience.

This book on *Emotional Resilience* will guide your development toward emotional mastery and resilience as you learn how your mind, emotions and physiology contribute to your automatic reactions. Together, we will explore how you can gain a greater sense of control over unexpected things that come your way, and how you can choose your response in ways that are empowering and life-affirming. You will learn how to:

- Explore how our core *values* drive our impulses, choices, decisions and actions consciously or unconsciously

- How our emotional reactions bubble up and produce emotional hijack
- Learn about Emotional Intelligence and take steps to improve it
- When you need to interrupt a pattern of ritualistic reactions that make you feel out of control
- Practice emotional regulation
- Develop mental toughness to enhance your resilience
- Use your body to manage your mental and emotional state

This book is an exploration of the mind, behaviour, emotions and the body and how all of these relate to enhance our emotional resilience.

In 2011 I published my first book on effective communication, *The Communication Chameleon*, which I use as a textbook for my courses at the University of Toronto and in professional career workshops. I have included three bonus chapters in this book because they offer expanded examples of many concepts I will discuss in this book. As you learn to explore your own emotional reactions and build your self-awareness and resilience, you will experience the personal transformation you seek.

You can read *Emotional Resilience* as a stand-alone manual on personal development, or pair it with *The Communication Chameleon*, which focuses on strategies for workplace success. Together, these two books will provide you with a comprehensive blueprint for rising above difficult situations and achieving your unlimited potential in both your personal and professional life.

CHAPTER ONE

Resilience

The word 'Resilience' comes from the Latin word 'resilio', which means 'to bounce back.'

Resilience is the ability to recover from difficulties quickly, to spring back and carry on. It is about having the skills and knowledge of how to cope and adapt after experiencing setbacks, obstacles and lack of resources. Resilience describes the capacity to function when facing stress, hurdles and difficult circumstances. It is an essential human quality which often determines how successfully you navigate through life.

Emotional Resilience combines resilience with the ability to recover from the strong negative emotions that frequently accompany a negative experience, and calm the mind. Throughout this book, the terms I use to discuss enhancing resilience are equally effective for enhancing emotional resilience, and I use them interchangeably.

We are surrounded by many examples of people who have demonstrated great resilience – Holocaust survivors, prisoners of war, and even people in your own life who may have overcome a traumatic experience. People who have navigated difficulties and obstacles beyond their control and found a way forward provide us with great examples of resilience and hope.

A famous inventor who is also a good example of a resilient person is Thomas Edison. As a child, teachers told him that he was 'too stupid to learn.' He was fired from multiple jobs for lack of productivity, and as an inventor of the light bulb, he had 1000 unsuccessful experiments before he hit on the right one. And yet his persistence and refusal to give up finally lead to a successful design that worked. Edison is known for saying "I have not failed. I've just found 10,000 ways that won't work."

Then there is Gertrude (not her real name), a 65-year old woman who became my client more than 10 years ago, and who is a wonderful example of resilience. She came to me to try out hypnotherapy in order to help alleviate the pain she was having throughout her body. Diagnosed with fibromyalgia, she was unwilling to spend the rest of her life taking pain medications and wanted to try something new.

When I met Gertrude she was taking weekly morphine injections and multiple Percocet painkillers each day. Our journey began with a conversation about her verbally and physically abusive husband, who she had divorced. One afternoon a couple of years later he knocked on her door, asked to talk and told her he was a changed man. When she asked him how he did it, he said ' I went from town to town, thinking things through, then something just clicked.' He told her that he realized he had lost the most important thing in his life because of his behaviour. He felt a burning desire to change – and he just did. After months of living together, she determined that he had indeed changed. She was so amazed at how much he had changed and that he really seemed like a new person. When he asked her to marry him again, she agreed.

In one session with Gertrude, I asked her if she had fully forgiven her husband. She thought about it for a few moments, and said, "In my head I think I forgive him, but sometimes the emotions come back." We discussed whether it was time to have a conversation with her husband about these unresolved feelings. She agreed that she still needed to confront him about the years of abuse. It took many conversations and apologies, before they were able to move past this period in their lives. At one point her entire body broke out in hives, and she described the experience as if she was shedding all the bad feelings she'd carried, while a great load had been lifted.

The next major situation we explored was the memory of a childhood experience she had growing up in Eastern Europe during wartime. One evening, as soldiers appeared in their village, all the adult females, including her older sister, hid underneath floorboards, in barns and other such places, for fear of assault. Since she was only 7 she was placed in bed under the covers when she vividly heard solders pounding at the door and her old grandmother answering. As she peered over the covers she could see two solders appearing, shouting and asking who is in the house. Her grandmother said just me and my little granddaughter who is asleep, pointing to the little cot in the corner of the room.

A soldier bounded across the room and dragged away the covers to see Gertrude huddled and trembling. She described how he glared at her with such evil eyes. Then he walked away, shoving the grandmother aside, overturning tables and chairs and looking underneath, grabbing food, before finally leaving. She said she cannot remember ever feeling such fear and terror, and how she had continued to tremble for what seemed to be hours. As she relived this trauma, I could see how disturbed she was, but she insisted that she didn't want to stop the process. Pushing through made her feel more empowered.

As a result of her persistence, Gertrude was able, over a period of months, to stop all morphine injections and only needed the occasional pain medication. Her doctor was shocked to see her progress and encouraged her by saying, "Keep on doing what you are doing!" Through the use of Hypnotherapy, self-hypnosis, emotional clearing, Neuro-Linguistic Psychology and cognitive and physical tools, for the most part Gertrude became pain-free. Her daily mantra continues to be 'I am pain-free.'

Gertrude's story is one of true resilience. Through all the challenges she endured, she kept her vision of having a healthy body, mind and emotions. She worked through layers of past experiences to regain her sense of well-being. She cultivated her resilience through having a clear goal of living without pain and she was willing to challenge many ingrained habits and thoughts that she felt limited her ability to get better.

We can all enhance our Emotional Resilience through building our knowledge and applying the **Resilience Four Factor Framework** in our lives. The four factors include Mental Toughness, Emotional Agility, Body Dynamics and Personal Mastery. These provide the foundational aspects for strengthening your resilience and building up your mental toughness.

Four-Factor Framework for strengthening your Emotional Resilience

1. **Mental Fortitude** – This is related to understanding your core values, enhancing

18

perseverance, challenging disempowering thinking, managing emotional responses and applying mindfulness.

2. **Emotional Agility** – This is related to your emotional intelligence (including your ability to release negative emotions) and emotional regulation. A linked component is emotional hijack and how it effects our thinking.

3. **Body Dynamics** – This is related to your physical body, your energy and how well your mind and body work together.

4. **Personal Mastery** – This is related to your self-awareness, self-esteem, ability to recognize and change behavioural patterns, and building a strong social network.

The materials covered here will provide you with a thorough understanding of the four factors and related tools to form a blueprint that you can follow to grow and cultivate your resilience.

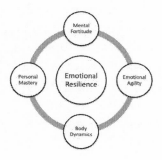

Mental Fortitude

*"To be yourself in a world that is constantly trying to make
you something else is the greatest accomplishment."*
— Ralph Waldo Emerson

Mental Fortitude refers to the perseverance, resilience and strength that people possess to break through their struggles in order to succeed. It is this mental toughness that gives us the ability to push past barriers, even to the point of exhaustion, in order to overcome whatever challenges that come our way.

Mental Fortitude is a trait that determines in large part how people deal with stressors and pressures, irrespective of the prevailing circumstances. Mental Fortitude is often considered resilience. When faced with adversity or tragedy some people seem to cope better; they adapt and bounce back quicker than others, while others appear stuck at that point, lacking the ability to advance or move forward.

We all have some degree of resilience, but until we actually encounter a very challenging situation, it's difficult to know if we possess the strength to get through it. Is your capacity to bounce back developed enough to help you through the most difficult periods in your life, situations where your level of stress doesn't overwhelm your internal resources? The good news is that we can all learn to increase our resilience and Mental Fortitude.

The newest research in neuropsychology has shown that the brain is neuroplastic. According to Oxford Dictionary, **Neuroplasticity** is the brain's ability to form and reorganize synaptic connections, especially in response to learning or experience or following injury. You can learn new coping strategies and more effective tools to deal with adversity due to your brain's ability to rewire itself.

How amazing is it to know that you can create new neural pathways through the experiences you are having each day? The secret to creating these new connections is repetition. I often tell students in my Psychology of Influence class at the University of Toronto that *"repetition creates belief."*

As you repeat a specific behaviour over and over, neurons in your brain fire over and over. Repetitive neural firing strengthens the connections in the brain to form new circuitry that support the behaviour or experience. Any elite athlete or professional musician can attest to the fact that practice makes perfect, and repetition is necessary to create the muscle memory and reflex response needed to perform under stress and pressure. This concept of repetition and reinforcement is the foundation of many of the tools and exercises discussed in this book.

Much of the behavioural change and new responses you will create in yourself with the tools introduced in this book will come from the automatic patterns that evolve from practicing a process over and over. Practicing a new response will build new tools of resilience, which become available to you in times of stress and challenge. In place of the often rigid kneejerk *reactions* we have to stress, neuroplasticity provides a way to build new, flexible *responses*. I specifically use the term **'reaction' versus 'response'** because when we **respond we are taking time to make a choice** of what behaviour we engage in, rather than showing an impulsive, automatic reaction.

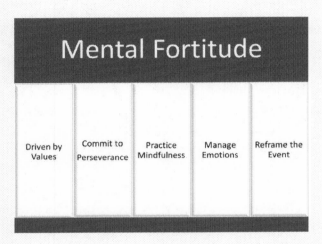

There are a number of factors that contribute to enhancing your Mental Fortitude. Through my experiences working with clients over the past two decades, I've identified four main factors that stand out as strong contributors to building mental resilience.

As depicted in the diagram above, there are five components to enhancing Mental Fortitude. Those with strong Mental Fortitude are **driven by values, demonstrate perseverance, manage their emotional reactions, practice mindfulness and reframe events** to help them respond effectively to difficult times.

Rather than allowing failure or stress to overwhelm you and drain your resolve, through the use of Mental Fortitude you can find a way to rise above it. Let's start with a discussion on how your core values contribute to creating a positive direction in your life.

Values Drive Behaviour

Values provide guidance for the way you live and work. These values drive behavioural impulses and decisions from deep in your subconscious. Values help you to determine priorities, and you use them to measure if your life is turning out the way you want it to be. Your values provide the framework for making choices that are good for you.

When what you do and how you behave match your values, life feels satisfying, instilling you with a sense of joy and contentment. On the other hand, if you are not living by your values or you are compromising your personal ideals, you will begin to feel frustrated and dissatisfied. This is the reason why making a conscious effort to identify your values, both personal and professional, is so important to living a fulfilled life.

Your values come from a variety of experiences, most of which are internalized from parents and familial rules and values of how to live, as well as from your schooling, religious and cultural practices. A person's life principles, personal ethics or standards of behaviour are developed from childhood experiences that reinforce specific attributes that become important. Over time, these values become the standards or ideals with which you evaluate actions, people, things or situations and how you make decisions for yourselves.

The values exercise at the end of this chapter offers a valuable process to learn about and document the ten most important values to you at this point in your life. This process can also be used with others around you, and even

23

your work team. Knowing one another's values provides us with a means to understand each other better and to know what is guiding our choices, decisions and behaviours.

Think of your values as subconscious needs which, when fulfilled, make you feel happier and more content. If they are not fulfilled, you may become frustrated, driven by subconscious impulses toward negative or self-destructive behaviours as you attempt to meet your needs.

For example, people who have an unfulfilled need for adventure might engage in overly-dangerous, thrill-seeking activities that might endanger them. Those who have a high need for personal connection and feel lonely might be drawn to risky intimate, short-term encounters. People who have a need for acceptance and affiliation but feel socially-isolated at work might engage in gossiping as a way to get attention and a sense of belonging.

Values Exercise

As it is with individuals, values also provide the guiding force for organizational behaviour. In the work I do with strategic planning, we always ensure early in the process that everyone in a workplace understands that the organizational **culture** is defined by **behavioural norms** which are based upon the **values** everyone has chosen to live by organizationally.

The following exercise is intended to establish a list of values for you and/or your team that will form the foundation to build a personally-fulfilling life and/or a high-performing team.

Instructions:

1. Make a copy of the attached values list for yourself, or to distribute among team members.

2. Each person circles or highlights their top 10 values from the list.

3. **The following steps are for the team process:** Everyone compares their lists to come up with the 6 values which you all have in common – this is your **team value list**.

4. Compare the team value list to the organizational values – every organization has their own mission, vision and organization values, which represent their mandate and unique culture. This is usually available on a company's website and employee handbook.

   How many matches do you see? The more matches there are between the organization's values and your own, the more alignment and cohesiveness there is in your team. There more alignment, the more cohesive and happy the team will be!

Values List
Circle your top ten values from the list below.

Accountability	entrepreneurial	patience
achievement	environmental	perseverance
adaptability	awareness	personal
ambition	ethics	fulfilment
ambiguity	excellence	personal growth
balance	fairness	professional
(home/work)	family	growth
being the best	financial stability	recognition
caring	forgiveness	reliability
clarity	friendship	respect
coaching/	future generations	risk-taking
mentoring	generosity	safety
commitment	health	security
community work	humility	self-discipline
compassion	humour/ fun	teamwork
competence	independence	trust
conflict resolution	initiative	vision
continuous	integrity	wealth
learning	job security	well-being
courage	leadership	(physical/
creativity	listening	emotional/
dialogue	making a	mental/ spiritual)
efficiency	difference	wisdom
enthusiasm	openness	
positive attitude		

Next, rank your 10 values in order of priority in the space below.

Living your Values Exercise

Now that you have your list of values, let's take a look at how they show up in your life. In the chart below, list your top 10 values in the Values column. Next, put a checkmark in columns one, two and/or three (professional, personal and social) where you feel you are living the value.

If you have rows with one or no checkmark beside any particular value, you will need to look at how to proactively create an experience or expression of the value.

Values	Work/ Career	Personal	Social	How will I enhance my experience of this value?

Commit to Perseverance

Mental Fortitude requires a commitment to persevere until the goal or result you are seeking has been achieved. In this process, you will need the ability to manage and overcome doubts, worries, concerns and any circumstances that might prevent you from succeeding or are hindering the outcome that you set out to achieve.

Think of the Wright brothers, the aviation pioneers who invented the world's first airplane. Can you imagine how many moments of heartbreak they must have had, how much sheer persistence kept them going before they finally achieved their vision of a machine in flight? The brothers battled depression and were plagued by family illnesses, but these challenges did not stop them from creating their first bicycle shop. The proceeds earned from this modest enterprise provided them the means to experiment with flight. After many years and many attempts at creating flying machines, after endless failed prototypes, the Wright brothers finally created a plane that could get airborne and stay airborne. They are a true example of perseverance.

Perseverance requires that you have a clear picture or vision of where you want to go and what you want to achieve. To make that happen, **goal-setting** is an essential part of developing the commitment that fires up your motivation to keep going, and maintaining a steady flow of effort toward the fulfilment of the goal.

Neuro-Linguistic Programming (NLP) is a term coined to describe the foundational belief that there are connections between the neurological and linguistic processes which form specific behavioural patterns that have been programmed in us based upon our life experiences. In Neuro-Linguistic Psychology, a technique for developing goals is a "well-formed intention." A central aspect of this technique is that the goal statement needs to be written in positive terms, in the present tense, and be highly sensory.

In order to ensure that you have a well-formed intention, I recommend using a slightly modified SMART goal. SMART goals are based on an acronym that means:

- **Specific** – Be specific. Instead of writing '*I want to lose weight*', you should write '*I want to lose 10 pounds.*'
- **Measurable and Motivational** – Losing 10 pounds is a measurable and realistic achievement. To make it motivational, don't start out with an extremely challenging target, like losing 100 pounds right off the bat, which would make it unrealistic. As you achieve each milestone, set a new goal of losing another 10 pounds. Make the goal more inspiring by writing about how great you will look and feel in your new wardrobe.
- **As if it is now** – this simply means that you should write your goal statement in the present tense, such as 'It is August 2019 and I have lost 10 pounds.' The subconscious mind does not experience time in a linear way, and also doesn't distinguish between what is imagined versus what is real.
- **Relevant** - this includes aspects that are specific and personalized to your goals. In other words, don't set goals for others, and set goals for yourself that are not contingent on other

people's participation; goals that you alone can have control over. If you depend on others to achieve your goal, they might not follow through.

- **Time-bound** and **Tangible**– pick a reasonable date when you feel you will complete the goal, and include this date in your SMART statement. A timeframe will create a sense of urgency. "Someday" is not a day on the calendar. Goal statements that include examples of the tangible experiences you will have when the goal has been achieved are more powerful, because the goal becomes grounded in all your senses. What will you see, hear and feel once the goal has been accomplished? The more sensory information you include in your goal statement, the more you will be motivated to get it done and the more information your subconscious has to work with in helping to manifest the goal.

Once you write down your SMART goal, it's time to focus all your attention on visualizing the goal as if it has already been achieved. I use a visualization process called Timeline Therapy™ with clients. This involves creating a vivid guided visualization where the client is taken on an imaginary journey – they see, hear and feel themselves as if the goal was already achieved, and it is inserted in their future timeline.

Visualization is just a fancy way of saying *Use your imagination!* Visualization has been proven to be a powerful way to **plant suggestions in the subconscious mind**. These suggestions become a template for the subconscious to filter reality such that we begin to see a way forward in actualizing the goal. The subconscious reacts to the impressions provided by the conscious mind and activates resources that help you to see potential steps you can take to move forward.

When you consciously visualize what you want, these images turn into **autosuggestions** that become planted in the subconscious. Once a suggestion has been embedded, various other systems are activated to fulfill these autosuggestions. One of these systems is the Reticular Activating System.

The **Reticular Activating System** (RAS for short) is a set of interconnected nuclei in the brain, connected to the spinal cord, which forms a series of circuits between the brainstem and the cortex. The RAS mediates the transitions from when you are in a relaxed wakeful state to periods of high attention. Visualization initiates your RAS to be on high attention, working to help you focus on those things that match with your autosuggestion and the goal.

When you create an intention in your conscious mind you activate the RAS, which heightens your awareness on a subconscious level, thereby helping you to notice more of what you want while suppressing other unwanted stimuli. The RAS spares you from having to process all the background "noise" by screening out irrelevant data not related to your goal. Simply put, you start seeing what you want to see. This is part of the reason why it is so important to focus on what you want by setting clear goals, rather than focusing on what you don't want.

I often work with clients to create a **picture collage** of their goal, which they post in a conspicuous place in their homes so that they can see it every day as a reminder of their goal. The collage is made up of images cut from magazines and pasted on cardboard.

Many years ago I had a dramatic example of the power of the picture collage. A client who was part of a women's coaching club I was running, made a large collage with various images to represent many of the key goals she wanted to achieve. A couple of years later she was happy to report that several of her goals had been accomplished, but with a peculiar twist. A number of the random images she had cut out to depict certain goals matched the goal exactly. One goal was to get a job in Europe. Eventually, after a number of applications to different European countries, she landed a job in England. Later, when she checked her collage, she noticed that she had cut out an image of London's Big Ben to represent having an overseas job. She didn't even remember choosing that image, but there it was! Several other images in her collage became uncanny matches for goals she eventually accomplished.

Manage Emotions

Managing your emotional responses to challenging or stressful situations is vital in keeping a rational mind that is not clouded by impulses or fear-based emotions. Having the skills to stay calm and control your level of anxiety in difficult and/or annoying situations is a key aspect of Mental Toughness. We will explore how to manage your emotions in more depth in the chapter on **Emotional Agility.**

Reframing

Reframing is a powerful tool for shifting your perspective of an experience by cognitively assigning another meaning to the experience. If you perceive something to be negative, you will experience a negative sensation in your physical and emotional state. Through reframing, you can use a different "frame of reference" to look at the same situation, in order to shift your reaction to it. We will cover a comprehensive review of reframing in the next chapter.

Shifting one's behavioural focus and asking different questions can lead to new realizations. Here are a few behavioural 'frames' that can shift your mindset:

- **Ask how** can I change this **rather than why** did this happen. "How" questions lead the mind to seek methods, while "Why" questions push you toward justifications and excuses. "How" also keeps us **focused on solutions** rather **than the problem.**
- Focus on **feedback** rather than **failure.** If you look at what has gone wrong as a learning opportunity that provides you feedback on how close or far you are from your desired outcome, you can move forward easier than if you dwell on the failure. Focusing on feedback is a way to keep the goal in mind, whereas focusing on failure leads to demotivation and hopelessness.
- **Build you confidence** by focusing on your successes. This will fill you with a sense of accomplishment and over time build up your confidence and a positive state of mind.

- **Take charge rather than wait.** Is there a current project that seems to be stagnating? How can you take charge or assemble a team to tackle the barriers? What are the primary action steps and resources needed to push things forward? Proactive people tend to feel a greater sense of control in their life. Being proactive helps to shift your **locus of control**.

  In 1954, psychologist Julian B. Rotter studied personalities and documented data about something he coined as the **locus of control**. In situations where a person feels they have control in their life, he or she is described as having an internal locus of control. An **external locus** is when a person believes that life is controlled by outside factors which he or she cannot influence.

In addition to these behavioural frames, I recommend a simple **visible tool** to shift your perceptions and locus of control.

Buy a Bristol board and draw a large circle on it. Hang the board in a prominent place where you can see it daily. Every day write down at least one positive note on a Post-it and stick it to the board. At the end of the month you have trained your brain 30 times to look for uplifting things. You can also do this exercise on social media, using the 30-day Challenge to post one daily thing you are happy or grateful for.

As you will learn in the Body Dynamics chapter, this simple task of focusing on one positive thing each day will rewire your brain to fire up more positive things on demand due to neuroplasticity.

It is critical for our well-being to have techniques that focus on the positive, given the fact that our minds have a **Negativity Bias**. As an evolutionary way to protect us from sudden danger, our brains have evolved to pay more attention to unpleasant, negative things than positive ones.

We are wired for fight or flight; however, while this ability served our prehistoric ancestors well during times of uncertainty, migration, hunting and foraging, it doesn't jive well with the challenges of 21st century living. The demands of modern society – which include fast-paced changes, long work schedules and family demands that deplete our down time and wreak havoc on our nervous system – leave us at increased risk of burnout and frustration.

As a result, negative thoughts, emotions, interactions and threatening events have a more intense impact on our emotional and psychological state versus positive things which have less impact on our emotions, behaviours and thoughts. A 2016 Psychology Today article titled 'Our Brains' Negative Bias,' reported a study where researchers interviewed couples and compared the number of arguments they had against the number of positive experiences the couples had in their relationships. The study found that a **five to one ratio of positive to negative experiences** among couples was necessary for them to have a satisfying relationship.

As a measure of your overall mindset, how many positive versus negative things did you think about today?

Now that we have covered the five components of Mental Fortitude, time to put together your action plan.

Learning in Action - Building Mental Fortitude

Use the following table to plan, set timelines and track your progress on each of the components.

Component / Tools / Process	Action Plan – Set a timeline for completing the tasks in the next 90 days. Track your notes below.
Complete the **Values Exercise** and Values Audit	
How are you l**iving the values**?	
Commit to perseverance with SMART goal-setting	
Visualize achieving your goals daily	
Create a **picture collage** of your goals	
Where could you use a new **behavioural reframe**?	
Remember to think about 5 positive things for every negative one.	
Read the Reframing Chapter and then write down what you want to reframe.	

CHAPTER THREE

Reframing: Creating New Meaning (Bonus Chapter)

Reframing is a powerful tool for shifting our perspective. You've probably heard people talk about someone's "frame of reference", where the individual's perspective provides a context or focal point for their thoughts and actions. Imagine the function of a picture frame: it creates the borders for an image. This is analogous to the **frame** a person might use to set the parameters of how they choose to view the world. These frames are defined by your beliefs about yourself and others. If you narrow your frame with limiting beliefs, you will reduce what you see in a situation. These limitations can be observed in "I can't do that" self-talk or "You can't do that" judgment of others.

When you are in a self-limiting frame, you have strong boundaries that are used to keep out anything that does not fit within the frame. A lot of my life coaching work is with individuals who hold beliefs which prevent them from exploring possibilities that are outside their frame of reference. Phrases such as "I am not promotable", "I will never get over these feelings of rejection" or "I can't learn these things, I'm too old," are all examples of limiting beliefs that lock the person away from the opportunity to test if these thoughts could indeed be false.

Typically, people don't question if their beliefs are true or false. They accept their beliefs as fact, holding that what they tell themselves has to be true. Time and again, I have witnessed how frames keep people stuck and incapable of letting go of a past experience that often creeps into the interactions they have with others.

When we reframe our perspectives, we see a situation from a different viewpoint. Reframing helps us to perceive, interpret, conclude and react to an experience in a different manner. Imagine being told that you have $200,000 versus $400,000 to buy an apartment – wouldn't it change your approach on where and what you buy? What about if you were told you had one week to work on a report versus two days? This timeframe would impact your level of stress and the method you would use to complete the report.

Reframing expands your potential by giving you another way to think, feel, do and ultimately choose how you will respond to an experience. Through reframing, you perceive new possibilities.

You can see reframing examples all around you. Many years ago a good friend told me a story about how he got to replace his living room windows. He kept telling his wife that he wanted to replace the windows, but at the time they just did not have the money. He kept pondering how he might raise the funds, and suddenly one summer afternoon a fluke storm came out of nowhere. Heavy winds and a dark, ominous cloud loomed just above his and a neighbour's house a few acres away. Within minutes, a shower of large hailstones fell down upon the houses, shattering several windows. My friend said that it was the oddest thing. While assessing the damage in the aftermath, he and his wife lamented their bad luck and wondered what they were going to do.

As quickly as the storm came, a thought came to him – *we are insured for this kind of problem! Yes, we can actually replace those old windows with the insurance money!* A month or so later they had brand new living room windows. Instead of thinking of the storm as the enemy, my friend considered it his good fortune, especially as their insurance premiums did not increase. This is a powerful example of reframing. He later told me, "My neighbour failed to reframe, even though he also used insurance to install new windows. My annoyed neighbour to this day still complains about the terrible storm that broke all of his windows, and he recreates the stress every time he tells the story."

We attach meaning to the events we experience due to our beliefs, values, biases and personal interpretations. You have probably heard two people having the same experience but describing it completely differently; this is the reason why when police arrive at the scene of an accident they quickly separate the witnesses and interview them independently.

So far we have been discussing **content reframing**, which answers the question *"What else could this mean to me?"* or *"In what way is this positive?"* We can also do **context reframing**. When we make a contextual change, we need to answer the question, *"In what context would this event or behaviour have value to me?"* If your best friend annoys you by never choosing the restaurants for outings, tell yourself *"Hooray, I get to pick what I want"* or *"They are easygoing enough to go along with my choice."* Trust me, the opposite can be worse – having someone who always wants to force their choice on you.

There are many applications of reframing in communication and counseling. These include:

• Difficult conversations

- Negative events
- Negative feelings and behaviours
- Limiting beliefs
- Options in negotiations
- Solutions to a problem

The Reframing Process

Reframing is one of the key tools described in detail by the founders of Neuro-Linguistic Programming, Dr. Richard Bandler and Dr. John Grinder, in their book *Frogs into Princes*. The process for reframing was described in six steps, which I have modified to be more applicable to reframing interpersonal interactions. Reframing can be achieved with the following procedures:

1. *Start with self-reflection to determine what negative behaviour you want to change. How does this behaviour make you feel? This is the awareness stage.*

2. *Imagine you are talking to the part of yourself that is producing this unwanted response. What purpose does the behaviour serve?*

3. *Relax and see if something comes to mind. In the chapter on "Formative experiences" we discussed that many negative behaviours are driven by a subconscious motivation that may have served a useful purpose or intention at some point in your past. However, this response may no longer serve you now.*

4. *Now, brainstorm on a piece of paper what you believe are alternative responses or meanings you could apply to the situation. Is it possible to develop a new behaviour that still serves the useful purpose? Can you see how a new response will have a more*

resourceful or positive result? This is the time to consider if a content or context reframe is required.

5. *Now evaluate each of the alternative responses. Which do you think would be the most natural and effective behavioural change that will help you to fully commit? You will need to allow yourself to accept a new perspective or response to the event in order to move past the old one.*

6. *Finally, review how the newly selected responses and/or meaning will affect you and others. Does the reframe make you feel a greater sense of well-being?*

Choosing between two negative options

Often we are faced with the unpleasant task of choosing between two equally unwanted alternatives. Reframing can help you to make the better selection. If you have a task that you find undesirable, you should contrast it with the consequence of not doing it. The ultimate objective is to allow yourself to see that the consequence of not completing the task is much more undesirable than doing the task in the first place.

Say you dislike tallying up all of your receipts each month in order to submit your expense report, so you typically procrastinate until the last minute. Now, your company has just implemented a policy that expense reports must be submitted in the same month that the expenses occur. If you are like me, your first reaction is frustration about the new policy, but once you settle down you will recognize that the consequence of your procrastination will be a loss of money, because you can't be reimbursed until those receipts are handed in. Sometimes it's all about choosing the lesser of two evils.

Reframe the situation so that *you* are making the choice, rather than feeling like you are being forced to do something you don't want. This puts the situation back under your control and helps you to see things in a more positive light. You will feel more powerful if you *choose* to do something rather than if you feel you *must* do it.

Follow the scheme below to help you reframe:
- You are told that *you must do X*, but you have told yourself that you don't want to
- So tell yourself that *if I don't do X, the consequence is Y*
- Therefore you willing *choose to do X to avoid the consequence Y*

Reframing can help to overcome negative events and generate hope for the future. It can also help people to picture a future state that is positive. The following story illustrates a situation where reframing has helped a client to feel more optimistic about her prospects.

My client was a lady who had just gone through a divorce and was feeling depressed about being a single parent and being alone. We used reframing to help her visualize a more positive future. In her visualizations, she was not longer controlled by her ex-husband's choices for her. She imagined doing all the fun activities she now had time for that she couldn't do before, and going on trips to places where her ex-husband hadn't wanted to go to. Instead of focusing on her loss, she focused on the exciting new possibilities that lay ahead.

Reframing will help you to unlock your inner potential as you transform your negative self-talk to be more uplifting.

CHAPTER FOUR

Emotional Agility

"Your heart knows the way. Run in that direction." – Rumi

Emotional Agility is all about noticing the moment-by-moment shifts in our feelings, without the impulse to express them. It entails taking control of your emotions and allowing yourself to experience a feeling, observe it, and choose whether or not you want to express it. Imagine a world where everyone is better at managing their emotions. How much better life would be if we all had clarity about our emotional triggers and stressors, if we learned how to choose our response, and could regulate emotions quickly and effectively in order to get back to a calm, rational state. This is Emotional Agility.

Emotional Agility is having a clear understanding of the concepts of Emotional Hijack, Survival Response, Emotional Intelligence and Emotional Regulation.

Emotional Agility

Emotional Hijack	Survival Response	Emotional Intelligence	Emotional Regulation

Are there certain situations where you feel like your emotions have taken control of you? **Emotional dysregulation** *is a term used in the mental health community to refer to emotional responses that are poorly modulated / exaggerated and do not lie within a socially acceptable range of emotional response.*

At a recent workshop for a not-for-profit organization, a participant explained that she felt very relaxed and in control at work, but totally *dysregulated* with her children. She expressed that it was no surprise to her that she acted this way, since her parents often had emotional outbursts. Subconsciously, a part of her believed this was a necessary part of parenting. I explained to her that she needed to challenge her beliefs in order to change this behaviour. She had to find and evaluate other methods of interacting with her family that didn't involve such volatile emotions.

Emotional volatility and mental health issues have become regular topics of conversations in lunchrooms, boardrooms and households. At every workshop I have taught over the past five years, there are at least two or three people who approach me to discuss mental health concerns for themselves, a colleague or a loved one.

The Institute for Health Metrics and Evaluation released its 2017 data on global mental health statistics, which revealed that 13% of the global population have a mental health disorder or suffer from substance abuse. This translates to 970 million people worldwide. The study further breaks down the stats to show that 3.4% have depression and 3.8% have an anxiety disorder, (https://ourworldindata.org/). Based on these numbers, there appears to be a growing mental health crisis which we urgently need to address.

Modern-day stressors

Think about the many stressors in your everyday life. Today's modern workplace presents a myriad perceived psychological stressors which can cause employees to experience a great deal of emotional distress, but few opportunities to openly talk about it.

We have more to do in less time; someone quits a position or goes on leave and we have to pick up the slack; gossiping and personality clashes are an unfortunate reality; colleagues are in competition with us for scarce resources or for the next promotion; we don't feel appreciated or rewarded for doing a good job, while others who put in less effort get the spotlight; sometimes there are rumours of downsizing.

These are common examples of external stressors that make us feel powerless. Then there are internal stressors that keep us up at night, such as a lack of confidence, social isolation, low self-esteem and feeling overwhelmed in keeping up with workloads or family commitments.

Instead of allowing the automatic emotional reactions to take hold of you, you can pause, take a deep breath and wait until the feeling passes. Next, think about the situation and choose how you want to respond to make things better for all concerned.

I know this is not easy when you're in the grip of emotional distress, but it is achievable. The process of understanding and managing your emotions starts with a discussion on emotional hijack and emotional regulation.

Emotional Hijack

What is the root of our stress response? Deep within our brain's limbic system is an almond-shaped mass of nuclei called the *amygdala*. This part of the brain plays a primary role in detecting threats and in the processing and storage of our emotional reactions. When we feel fear or stress, the fear stimuli is processed via the amygdala through the Hippocampus, where the stimuli is compared with a past memory and a survival response is elicited – fight, flight or freeze.

The fight or flight symptoms are accompanied by a series of physiological and psychological responses. We experience rapid heartbeat, increased blood pressure and shallow breathing, all happening as stress hormones such as cortisol are flooding into our bloodstream. These are all natural reactions that we would experience if we were under physical danger, yet these hormones are released in response to workplace stressors.

When we have a stressful experience it can be fear-producing, such as someone's negative tone of voice rising as they demand something from you, or a reproachful look from your manager. The amygdala takes over and fires off the **survival response (fight and flight),** along with the accompanying emotional reactions. At the same time, the logical, rational part of the brain, the prefrontal cortex, goes offline.

This cascade of responses that arises when the amygdala takes charge of our behaviour is called **Emotional Hijack.** The **prefrontal cortex** – which is required for more complex thinking and analysis – is dampened by the amygdala's response. The prefrontal cortex is the brain region involved in complex cognitive behaviours, personality expression, decision-making and moderating social behavior.

Another way to look at this process is that the **fear reaction essentially prevents our rational thinking,** leading us to interpret a situation in ways that dramatically skew our perception of reality. We become defensive and hypersensitive to what is happening around us. Rational thinking becomes muddled and confused when we are experiencing intense emotion, and the possibility of misinterpreting the situation becomes very likely.

Take a moment for self-reflection.
What are some external and internal stressors that may be causing emotional hijack for you?

My external stressors are:

My internal stressors are:

A case of Emotional Hijack

A client (let's call him John) visited my office to discuss a situation he was having at work. John indicated that his boss would often ask him at the last minute if he could stay late to help finish up reports. Because of these unpredictable requests, there were a number of times when he missed all or parts of important family events. When

John first started working there, he didn't mind complying since he wanted to make a great impression and show his boss his great work ethic. Six months later, however, it became clear that his boss was not going stop the last-minute requests.

It got to be that when his boss asked for something, my client would just nod and storm away silently, feeling angry. By the time John arrived home he was very short-tempered with his wife and kids. He had already tried to give his boss non-verbal hints (shrugging his shoulders, grimacing and holding his head down), but his boss didn't notice these subtle cues. John now felt helpless to change the situation since his boss appeared to think it was ok to saddle him with last-minute projects all the time.

As we reviewed the situation, I asked John if he had ever told his boss that he couldn't keep staying late at work on short notice. He answered, "No, I can't find a way to tell him." I indicated to him that since a lot of time had passed without addressing the issue, his boss had probably come to regard such expectations as reasonable and would continue to make eleventh hour requests.

My client needed to see that by not speaking up and asserting a boundary, he had inadvertently contributed to his own problem. By freezing up and not explaining, he was adding to his own emotional hijack. John's inability to speak up and make his feelings clear is a typical flight response. Instead, he internalized his dissatisfaction and ended up taking it out on his family.

So what was the remedy to his dilemma? We reviewed and rehearsed what he could say to his boss. John needed to "interrupt the pattern" of his automatic reactions of ignoring the problem. Naturally, he was very nervous about what his boss's reaction might be if and *when he expressed his true feelings, but he realized that he had to grow more assertive and find the courage to make a conscious effort and stand up to his boss.*

I advised him to discuss the matter before another last-minute request was made, because it would probably be much more difficult to break the pattern in that very moment.

The very next day, John asked his boss for a brief meeting just after lunch (a good time to have conversations because the person is more likely to be in a "satiated" state). John started by thanking his boss for taking a few minutes out of his busy day to have the conversation, then took a deep breath and repeated what we had rehearsed.

"I feel responsible for misleading you about my short notice availability. For the past six months I promptly agreed to stay late on short notice, even on days when I've made plans with my family, and I never told you that it was becoming more and more stressful to keep breaking plans with them. I notice that I've become more and more upset about this. I really enjoy working here and with you, and I don't want this to affect how I feel about my job. I am hoping we can work together to plan ahead for the days you will need me to stay a little later, and this way I can create a better work/life balance."

When he recounted his story, he said that the entire time he was speaking, his hands were sweating and he felt nervous, but the more he expressed how he felt, the more relieved, relaxed and confident he felt. When he was finished he stayed silent and waited for his boss' reaction.

To his surprise, his boss apologized for taking him away from his family and said he had not realized that his employee was stressed. They both committed to be more forthcoming with each other about how things affected them. His boss agreed that he would definitely work with him to improve timing and plan ahead for project tasks so that he would have more lead time where possible.

John was very grateful that his boss was so understanding. He was shocked that he hadn't said something earlier and had allowed things get to this point. He finally realized how important it is to address behavioural issues early on, so that patterns of expectations don't form and get muddled. He also acknowledged his implicit compliance with his boss' demands through his own "flight behaviour."

How many times have you avoided addressing the behaviour of someone who has caused you to feel upset, because of your own flight behaviour or fear of conflict? Have you ever walked away at the moment something happened only to blow up at the person much later, causing the other individual to be surprised that you were even upset? With emotional regulation you can train yourself to respond calmly and assertively, letting them know how their behaviour negatively impacted.

Emotional Intelligence

We often fear talking about our feelings, especially in the workplace. We don't want those around us to think we are unprofessional or emotionally sensitive. So, we tend to supress our feelings to work. Research in organizational psychology has established that *emotional intelligence* is essential for employee effectiveness at all levels in the organization, and is a common key factor taken into consideration when evaluating workers for promotion.

Emotional intelligence (EI) can be defined as the skill and ability to identify, assess and control the emotions of oneself and others. The roots of emotional intelligence can be traced to Charles Darwin's work on the importance of emotional expression for survival and adaptation. In 1920, E.L. Thorndike used the term *social intelligence* to describe the skill of understanding and managing other people. Similarly, in 1940 David Wechsler described the influence of non-intellective factors on intelligent behavior, and further argued that our models of intelligence would not be complete until we can adequately describe these factors.

In 1983, American psychologist Howard Gardner introduced the idea of multiple intelligences. These included both **interpersonal intelligence** (the capacity to understand the intentions, motivations and desires of other people) and **intrapersonal intelligence** (the capacity to understand oneself, to appreciate one's feelings, fears and motivations). In Gardner's view, traditional types of intelligence assessment tools such as IQ tests fail to fully explain cognitive ability, performance outcomes and the promotion-readiness of individuals.

In 1998, renowned researcher and writer on emotional intelligence Daniel Goleman introduced a model that breaks EI into a list of core competencies and skills. Goleman's model has five EI competencies, including self-awareness, self-regulation, motivation, empathy and social skills. One of the models I use in my EI workshops has five similar competencies, which I've listed and defined in this chart.

Related To	Competency and Definition
Emotional Intelligence - **Self**	1. **Self-awareness** – The ability to recognize and understand your moods, emotions and drives, as well as their effect on others.
Emotional Intelligence - **Self**	2. **Self-regulation** – The ability to control or redirect disruptive emotional impulses and moods; the propensity to suspend judgment and think before acting.
Emotional Intelligence - **Self**	3. **Motivation** – A passion to work based on an internal drive or propensity to pursue goals with energy and persistence.
Emotional Intelligence - **Others**	4. **Social Awareness** – The ability to understand the emotional makeup of other people and how your words and actions affect others
Emotional Intelligence - **Others**	5. **Social regulation** – The ability to influence the emotional clarity of others through a proficiency in managing relationships, diffusing conflict and building networks.

Goleman believes that emotional competencies are not innate talents, but learned capabilities that must be worked on and developed to achieve outstanding performance. He asserts that individuals are born with a general emotional intelligence that determines their potential for learning emotional competencies.

A significant aspect of my consulting work is to perform Emotional Intelligence assessments for private and corporate clients. These assessment reports provide a list of top competencies and an Emotional Quotient score, which is a measure of a person's overall emotional intelligence. This report is then used as roadmap for professional coaching and development programs.

In my experience, individuals can improve their emotional intelligence if they are willing to actively work on building the emotional intelligence competencies defined in the chart above – self-awareness, self-regulation, motivation, social regulation and social awareness.

Let's explore these each of competencies further.

Self-awareness

Introspection is the process of examining our thoughts, feelings, behaviours and motives. **Self-awareness** requires a level of introspection that most of us typically don't engage in. Through introspection, our examination of ourselves can lead to a better understanding of our personality and individuality. We start to learn about the characteristics that others see in us.

Self-Awareness Theory states that noticing ourselves and our behaviour leads us to judging our behaviour according to an internal standard. This standard helps us to maintain our self-image. Those who are self-aware recognize their values, strengths, weakness and motivators. They know their own feelings and how they tend to react in various situations. Self-awareness is essential for everyone, especially for those in leadership roles. Participants of my leadership programs undergo comprehensive analysis in order to develop a keen sense of themselves and how their behaviour impacts those around them.

We talk about **emotional contagion,** which is a phenomenon where one person's emotion triggers a similar emotion in those around them. We unconsciously mirror and match one another's behaviours and emotions. Leaders have a duty to manage their emotions and actions in a way that does not negatively affect their staff.

As individuals, we also have a duty to be cognizant of the impact of our behaviour on friends and loved ones. Increasing one's self-awareness is a tool for developing an understanding of this impact. We can build insights through self-reflection, journaling, and taking personality assessments.

Self-regulation

Self-regulation involves controlling one's behaviour, emotional reactions, and thoughts in order to effectively pursue our goals and desires. We take charge of and feel responsible for our actions without the influence of any external pressure. A common example might be making the conscious choice to limit the amount of time spent watching TV or surfing the Internet in order to have the time to go for a walk.

In the context of developing emotional intelligence, we are focusing on **emotional self-regulation**; this is a critical aspect of self-regulation and refers to the ability to manage disruptive emotions and impulses. Self-regulation means that you don't verbally attack others or make rush, emotional decisions. Along with identifying your values and emotional triggers and engaging in mindfulness practices, making the time to pause and take a deep breath before reacting to a situation is an effective way to start managing our emotions.

Motivation

For the purpose of increasing emotional intelligence, we define **motivation** as a passion to work diligently based on an internal drive, or the propensity to pursue goals with energy and persistence.

In motivational needs theory, motivation is described as intrinsic or extrinsic. **Intrinsic motivators** are factors that drive our behaviour from within (personal interests and desires) and **extrinsic motivators** are factors that drive our behaviours due to external factors such as inspiration from others, praise, or tangible rewards such as a paycheque or prize. We should also add that people are driven to fulfill their personal and family-related goals in order to thrive as an individual. Setting goals, being hopeful and optimistic are general ways to maintain motivation.

A useful model to help us understand motivational needs is called the McClelland Theory of Needs, otherwise known as the acquired-needs theory. In this theory, psychologist David McClelland describes three primary categories of needs that motivate people: **the need for achievement, for affiliation, and for power**. McClelland believes that people grow into these needs depending upon their life experiences. Their motivation and effectiveness on the job is based upon how the job allows the individual to experience fulfillment of these needs.

The three motivational needs are:

Need for achievement – The drive to excel and achieve beyond a set of defined standards, and to have success.

Need for power – The need to influence others to move toward a goal and to be in charge of specific objectives.

Need for affiliation – The desire for friendly and close interpersonal interactions.

To nurture these motivational factors in ourselves and others, using the workplace as an example, we should follow these guidelines:

- *Employees with a high achievement need* should be put in positions where they will have challenging but achievable tasks. They will need regular verbal and written feedback, recognition and credit for their accomplishments. These individuals don't mind working on their own.

- *Employees with a high affiliation need* should be put in positions where there is opportunity for team work and cooperative situations. These individuals don't mind frequent interactions with the public.

- *Employees with a high power need (specifically institutional power)* should be provided opportunities to lead and manage others. These individuals will be comfortable taking on the responsibility to influence others toward a goal.

Social Awareness

Social Awareness is the ability to understand the emotions of others, to emphasize with others and be aware of how our words and actions affect others. We need to watch out for **cognitive bias**, which is the tendency to process and filter information through the lens of our own experiences, likes and dislikes. It is especially prevalent during arguments, when we become increasingly incapable of accurately processing what the other person is trying to make us understand. An individual who is socially aware uses highly-developed social skills such as effective communication and conflict resolution to truly connect and learn about those around them. The social art of expressing appreciation and giving praise are vital aspects for someone who is socially aware and who is capable of interacting with others in a positive and inspiring manner.

Social Regulation

Social Regulation is the ability to influence the emotional clarity of others through a proficiency in managing relationships, diffusing conflict and building networks. This competency requires that a person have **behavioural flexibility** to effectively interact with others in order to build **rapport** and long lasting relationships.
The chart below shows the five competencies, along with a variety of tools for enhancing them.

Attribute / Competencies	Development - Tools & Concepts
Self-awareness	- Self-reflection & journaling - Ask others how they see you - Understand formative experiences - Understand self-identity factors - Body Dynamics, body-based tools
Self-regulation	- Emotional Agility - Reframing - Practicing emotional regulation - Body Dynamics, body-based tools - Interrupt-the-pattern & Power Pose
Motivation	- Resilience & Persistence - Building Mental Fortitude - Living your values - SMART goal-setting - Challenge limiting beliefs

Social Awareness	- Emotional Literacy - Emotional Intelligence - Emotional Regulation - Personal Mastery - Resolve Conflict
Social Regulation	- Emotional Intelligence - Emotional Regulation - Develop Personal Mastery - Behavioural Flexibility - Build Rapport - Resolve Conflict

Emotional Literacy

The term **emotional literacy** and the phrase "emotional intelligence" have been used interchangeably. The term *emotional literacy* was first used by French psychotherapist Dr. Claude Steiner, who defined it as *"the ability to understand your emotions, the ability to listen to others and empathize with their emotions, and the ability to express emotions productively."*

In a 1997 article, Dr. Steiner argued that *"To be emotionally literate is to be able to handle emotions in a way that improves your personal power and improves the quality of life around you. Emotional literacy improves relationships, creates loving possibilities between people, makes co-operative work possible, and facilitates the feeling of community."*

Steiner believes that at its core, emotional literacy is about understanding your feelings and those of others in order to facilitate relationships, and this includes using dialogue and self-control to avoid negative arguments. The ability to be aware of and to read other people's feelings optimizes your communication skills and enhances your interactions with others, in a phenomenon that Steiner describes as *emotional interactivity*. By looking inwards Steiner argues that personal power can be magnified to transform relationships in in all areas of your life.

Emotional literacy can be broken down into five parts:

1. ***Know your feelings*** - *This means you are aware of your sensibilities and when your 'buttons' are being pushed, and are able regulate your reaction. Are you too self-critical, self-doubting or having too much negative self-talk?*

2. ***Have a sense of empathy*** - *Empathy is the ability to understand and share the feelings of another, to step into their shoes and relate to the experience they are having. This is developed through building behavioural flexibility and unbiased, deep listening.*

3. ***Learn to manage emotions*** - *This is about your capacity for emotional self-regulation, and is developed through emotional regulation techniques, Mindfulness practices, and enhancing your Personal Mastery.*

4. ***Repair emotional damage*** - *This is related to interrupting patterns of emotional reactions that are disempowering, and re-conditioning your mind with repeated exposure to new experiences that make you feel more powerful and in control. Practicing Mindfulness will also help to alleviate symptoms of anxiety and stress.*

5. ***Emotional interactivity*** - *The ability to be aware of and to read other people's feelings optimizes your communication skills and enhances your interactions with others.*

Psychologists are now advising that Emotional Intelligence plays a far greater role in career success and job performance than just IQ (cognitive ability). Recent studies have shown that emotional intelligence is a better predictor of a person's suitability for promotion than the numerical result of a conventional IQ test.

A meta-analysis study of 69 independent studies explored the predictive validity of emotional intelligence with diverse job performance outcomes (Van Rooy, 2004) and found correlations that suggest emotional intelligence can be considered a moderate predictor of job performance and success, relative to other types of personnel selection techniques – including interviews and personality inventories. Additional findings derived from emotional intelligence research studies reveal that:

- Employees who lack social and emotional intelligence perform more poorly than those who scored high in conscientiousness and emotional intelligence.
- The highest-performing managers and leaders have significantly more "emotional competence" than other managers.
- Poor social and emotional intelligence are strong predictors of executive and management derailment and failure in one's career.

Given the immense body of research that has been produced over the last few decades, it is clear that Emotional Intelligence is not something that can be overlooked or neglected. If we want to succeed in our personal and professional lives, we need to increase our Emotional Intelligence. As a result, we will be able to express our emotions in a more constructive manner as well as have the skills to build strong social connections.

Tools for Change

Understanding **emotional hijack** and **emotional intelligence** are critical for success because you get to appreciate the impact these factors have upon your performance, well-being and relationships. Past emotional experiences and their accompanying reactions can cause you to react to a present situation as if you were actually re-experiencing the past. Even when the present situation is only an approximation of the past event, you may still recycle the same response, which is likely inappropriate to the present situation. Learning emotional regulation is the antidote to breaking such cycles of habitual responses.

Emotional Regulation

Emotional regulation is the ability to respond to a wide range of emotions in a manner that is socially acceptable and flexible enough to have an immediate or delayed reaction, as the situation requires. Emotional regulation can be enhanced via in a variety of methods. Emotional self-regulation decreases exposure to unwanted emotions while increasing emotional resilience in the event that such emotions do come up. Developing skills to manage your emotions will help you to prevent emotional reactions that may create difficulties. The following are various methods for developing self-regulation skills:

- Create new experiences to generate new emotional responses
- Change how you express yourself to others
- Avoid triggering situations while you practice how to shift your emotional response
- Practice mindfulness

61

- Use / shift your body to interrupt behavioural patterns
- Reframe to create new meaning

Mind Hacks – how to create new experiences to generate new emotional responses

Neuropsychology research shows us that our nervous system's pathway of responses is shaped by our experiences. This is due to neuroplasticity, as covered in the Mental Fortitude chapter. Through repetition of an activity, we can condition new responses and learn new coping strategies, as well as become more flexible in our responses.

Exercise: write down three things you did well each day – in 30 days you will have 90 entries that will build up your confidence and self-esteem.

Another mind hack is to practice and mentally rehearse what you will do differently if you encounter a stimuli that typically causes you to react in a thoughtless manner.

Exercise: the next time someone upsets you, instead of blowing up in anger, walk away. Next, take a few deep breaths and write down what you would say if you weren't angry. Repeat the message a few times to yourself, then approach the person and share the specifics of what they did and how it made you feel.

Changing how you express yourself to others

When we try to express emotions, we might say something like, "You made me angry when you said I wrote a bad report." The problem with this statement is that it instantly creates defensiveness in the other person. It sends them right into their own emotional hijack and renders them unable to reason with us. In addition, by starting an accusatory sentence with the word "You", you blame the entire person for your emotional reaction, which is somewhat inaccurate and makes it impossible for them to figure out what they specifically need to change to make things better.

The other person may have triggered a negative emotion within you, but you still have a **choice** in how you will respond. When we get upset, we typically react by expressing our emotions in a non-constructive way rather than in a **relaxed, assertive** manner. To be relaxed and assertive means that you are in full control of your response, and you are mindfully expressing yourself. Recognize that you may or may not get acknowledgement from the other person, but you do not need to be afraid to assert a clear boundary around how you wish to be treated.

As an alternative, you could say *"When you used that tone of voice and told me that my report was bad, I felt disrespected."*

Let us deconstruct this message to illustrate why it is a more accurate way of expressing how you are feeling:

First, you have **identified the specific behaviour and words** that caused you to feel disrespected; this makes it easier for the other person to change. Also, you **own your emotion** when you say "I felt", which is another way of coaching yourself to take control of your reaction. **Relaxed-assertive** means that you have expressed yourself in a controlled state, which can now lead to a **constructive conversation** where the other person is less defensive and thus more able to really hear what you are saying.

Overcoming physical responses

Having constructive interaction with someone is only possible if you and the other person are not under an emotional hijack. *But what happens if you are already under emotional hijack? What do you do to get out of it?*

As discussed earlier, when we lose emotional control over a situation, we are experiencing not just the stressful emotions but also undergoing a fight-or-flight response which impacts our physical feelings and reactions. Thus, when encountering a stressful situation, we need to immediately do something to overcome both the physical and the psychological effects of the emotional hijack.

Here is my recommendation: think about the physical experiences you might have when you are angry – a flushed face, holding your breath or clenching your teeth. Until you reduce these symptoms, you will be unable to think clearly. The first step toward alleviating these physical reactions is to take a few deep breaths and focus on moving your conscious attention into your body – relax your muscles and unclench those fists and teeth.

A tip I often give my clients is to wiggle their toes inside their shoes, to walk away or silently count backwards from 100 until they regain sufficient emotional control. Such activities go far toward reducing nervous-system reactions and bringing us back to higher levels of thinking, where we can make rational decisions.

Shifting emotional response patterns

Once you have overcome a negative physical reaction, you must direct your attention to your feelings. Over the years I've learned that it is impossible to have a rational conversation if you have not acknowledged and validated the intense emotions that are present.

People want to know that you understand how they feel before they are able to move on. The second step in overcoming an emotional situation is to listen and acknowledge the other person's feelings and to express and validate your own.

One way to figure out how others are feeling is to ask, "Can you please share with me how you feel about this situation. I really want to understand what I can do to make things better." By inquiring into another person's feelings, we might find out that they are upset about the specific words we have used, our tone of voice, or something we did physically. These are all behaviours that we can work to change.

We can express empathy for how the other person feels without being pressured into apologizing for something we don't feel we did wrong, which may lead to resentment in the long run. It is important to distinguish between our feelings of empathy because someone is hurt, versus agreeing with their perspective on why they are hurt.

Imagine that someone has unintentionally done something to hurt you. You respond by raising your voice or using unkind words because you feel hurt. Rather than helping the situation, your emotional reaction becomes a distraction in the conversation, because now the other person feels justified for being angry. By yelling at them, the focus has moved away from their behaviour to yours.

In this situation, we can be sorry for raising our voice and apologize without having to agree with the other person or condone their behaviour. You need to make an attempt to clarify the difference, and you can do so by

65

saying: "I am sorry that what I said hurt you. I apologize for raising my voice AND I do want to discuss how I was also hurt by what happened."

Is it easy to control our emotional reactions?

No, emotional control is not easy, especially if you have an established pattern of response with a particular person. This pattern of response leads to the ritualistic acting out of each step in the pattern. However, by building up your self-awareness, you can begin to catch yourself before you repeat the behaviour you hope to change.

It is important to be patient with yourself as you start to make these changes. Automaticity is working against you. You're working against the grain, fighting back against the impulse to reach for the familiar, and duplicate a set of behaviours that are not doing you any favours at present. But naturally your subconscious wants to repeat the programmed response. When you catch yourself slipping back into such a pattern, gently remind yourself to STOP the old behaviour. Then immediately fill yourself with the new behaviour you are substituting for the old.

Below is a summary of steps you can use to interrupt negative emotional patterns:

1. *Develop self-awareness of your own emotional pattern through self-reflection, or by asking family and friends to help you notice the pattern.*

2. *Catch yourself just before, during, or even after performing the old response.*

3. *Tell yourself that you have chosen to STOP this behaviour. This will cause you to subconsciously pay more attention to the ways you tend to react.*

4. *Deal with the physical symptoms of the fight-or-flight response by breathing deeply, walking away, counting backwards or wiggling your toes.*

5. *Immediately catch yourself and mentally rehearse or act out the replacement behaviour. Remember that repeating the new experience will create new neural pathways that support the new response.*

6. *Practice the new pattern over and over until it becomes an automatic habit.*

Please note: a final action plan chart is not provided here because the learning in action steps are included throughout the chapter, and there are also references to exercises and tools found throughout the book.

CHAPTER FIVE

Formative Experiences and Anchors (Bonus Chapter)

Our childhood formative experiences contribute to the main components of our core belief system. These beliefs become the foundation of how we interpret external stimuli and perceive our reality. Many of our subconscious habits and aspects of our self-image are laid down during our formative years – and by this I mean not only our developmentally-formative years (birth to age ten), but also the first encounters that come to form the foundation of our belief system – the friends we have in school, the social and community groups we belong to, our first love and our first job.

Many of our everyday reactions to stressful situations, as well as patterns of behaviour, can come up automatically, without any need for thinking. Our mind is efficiently designed to take in as much information as possible and store it for future use without the need for us to process it consciously at all. These subconscious patterns can work for us or against us, depending on whether the resulting behaviour is constructive or destructive.

Several years ago, a client came to me to help her overcome one such subconscious pattern, what she called her addiction, to a well-known Canadian coffee shop chain. Every time she drove past one of these shops, she instantly felt the urge to drive in and buy a coffee. Over time she became very concerned about the amount of caffeine she was consuming every day, so we worked together to design a hypnotic script that would have her substitute herbal tea for coffee.

After three sessions of hypnosis, she began to see results. Now each time she entered this coffee shop, she would order herbal tea. However, she began to experience another peculiar behaviour every time she bought the tea: she would ask to have a lot of cream added, just like when she had ordered the coffee. She realized that she never before had any cream or milk in her tea, but now that she no longer bought coffee, she really craved the cream.

As she relayed this behaviour to me, I instantly recognized that her addiction was actually to the cream rather than the coffee. I asked her, "When did cream become so important to you?" She looked at me in a puzzled way. "What do you mean?" she asked. I repeated, "Think back, when did eating cream become significant in your life?" She suddenly burst into tears and told me the following story.

Growing up we used to receive fresh milk in bottles that were left at our door step. I would race home ahead of everyone else so that I could scoop the cream off the top of the milk and eat it. It was so delicious and it was all for me. I would feel so good, peaceful and safe for about a half-hour before my siblings and parents came home. My dad was an alcoholic and when he came home at dinner time, there was always fighting in the house. He would shout and swear at my mother and all of us children.

I informed her that the cream had become a **subconscious psychological anchor**, a connection to the feelings of being safe and at peace. Whenever she felt any stress pop up in her life, her subconscious guided her back to the cream to recreate these positive feelings as a coping mechanism. In essence, the cream was the stimuli and the response was the happy feelings she gained as a result. It became clear to her that she needed to find ways to create positive feelings without having to consume large quantities of cream.

Through additional sessions she gained further insights into how her formative experiences were triggering many of her reactions to others, including her sometimes angry outbursts. We worked together as she developed a number of new behaviours and responses that helped her to manage her stress and not turn to old patterns for comfort.

Let's take a closer look at what happened here. We see that formative experiences can subconsciously drive our behaviour without our knowledge. These past events create associations between a specific event and a particular state of being.

In this case, when stressed as a child my client started pairing the eating of the cream with the positive emotions of being in control, feeling peaceful and safe. Many years later, her stress retriggered the association, and she reached for the cream. A typical stimulus-response pairing was now in charge of her actions. Stimuli-response pairings are triggered by **anchors**. In this case, the anchor was the stress my client was feeling, which triggered the need to relieve it by consuming cream.

I witnessed another powerful case of anchoring in a client whom I will call Jim. Jim was referred to me by a good friend whom I had worked with many years earlier. Jim told me that whenever he went to parties, he would suddenly develop very sad feelings. He had thought about it many times, but could not determine what would cause this shift in his emotional state. He would be having a great time, when out of nowhere he would get hit with a sense of overwhelming sadness.

I asked him to replay, step-by-step, the most recent party he could remember attending where he had this emotional shift occur.

"Well," he said, "I remember we were all sitting around in my brother's backyard, just having beers and burgers and chatting. An old family friend arrived and walked around just shaking hands, saying hi to everyone. When he got to me, he gave me a friendly tap on the shoulder and asked how things were. As I began to tell him how great everything was, I could feel a shiver go up my back. In no time, a wave of sadness was running through me. I got up to leave soon thereafter, but my brother stopped me and asked why I was leaving so early. I did what I always do when I make my escape – snap at him to let me go, and tell him I was too busy to stop and explain myself."

Jim continued to describe how this cycle of sadness – becoming short-tempered, then snapping at others – was a standard part of his communication repertoire, especially with his family. He really wanted to figure out what was going on so that he could repair his relationship with his brother and other family members.

I knew that I needed to look for the anchor (i.e. stimulus) that was triggering his reaction. He described another event, and I started to notice a common thread. In each case there was a moment where **someone would tap him on the shoulder.** I asked him, *"Do you remember a time in the past when you were tapped on the shoulder, over and over again?"*

71

He looked perplexed for a moment. "Why would you ask me that?"

I responded by asking, "Why, do you remember something?"

Tears suddenly began to stream down his face. He said, "Yes, I remember being 14 years old and sitting in the foyer of our house. Everyone who came in walked over to me, tapping me on the shoulder and saying, Sorry about your mom, everyone misses her but it will be ok." His mother had just died and this was the reception after the funeral.

After Jim composed himself, I showed him how being tapped on the shoulder was associated with the sadness he was feeling at that moment; essentially, the tapping became an anchor. Every time someone tapped him on the same shoulder it brought back the sad feelings, particularly during a party-like atmosphere where family and friends were present. The combination of the sitting and the tapping were triggering his emotional shift, which in turn caused him to snap or completely shut down and stop communicating with the people around him.

Jim had not fully completed the grieving process for his mother and so his sadness was suppressed, only to surface when triggered with the tap on the shoulder.

Tools for change

Jim and I worked together to successfully replace the anchor. Replacing an anchor involves a technique called **"collapsing or squashing the anchor."** In Jim's case, the anchor was both unknown to him and unintentionally created to elicit a negative response (anchors that are unintentionally created are called *natural anchors*).

To squash the anchor, we needed to intentionally create a new, powerful positive anchor which would be used to counteract the negative one. **I did it by tapping him on the opposite shoulder, while asking him to remember many positive memories in order to get him to reach an ultra-positive emotional state.**

The process then required that both anchors be triggered together. This meant tapped him on the left and the right shoulder simultaneously, so that over time the positive feeling would neutralize the negative one. Triggering both anchors initially caused Jim to have very mixed feelings, but after several applications the tapping of the left shoulder no longer produced sensations of sadness. Jim also worked on bringing closure to his mother's death.

So far we have illustrated how our formative experiences contribute to our programmed of subconscious behaviours. It is vital to gain a clear understanding of how your past has embedded subconscious anchors that trigger specific reactions in you. Then look at how they are related to your interactions with others.

We have observed the importance of our formative experiences and anchors as a way to learn more about ourselves and the subconscious processes that drive our behaviours when we communicate with others. On your road to discovery, you will gather an inventory of triggers and situations that might lead to difficult conversations. There are a variety of tools that can help you to break free of such deeply-ingrained negative habits. I have already written about *pattern interrupt* and *squashing anchors* as great tools for breaking habits.

Anchors can also be intentionally set to be used to your advantage. Physical cues can be utilized to interrupt a pattern and elicit a more positive, desired state. Here are a few examples:

o   **Example 1:** Every time you dance, snap your fingers when you are in a positive state. The snapping fingers will become an anchor to being in an excited state. The next time you feel a bit down or tired, stand up, take a deep breath and snap your fingers to rekindle the euphoria of when you were dancing.

Some people habitually and subconsciously make a certain movement with their body when they are in a particular emotional state. Observe how someone behaves when they are happy: what are their habitual gestures? You can build rapport – a positive connection – by imitating this habit. You might just cause them to jump back into that happy state.

I have seen an example of this with a salesperson with whom I worked in the past. He would always rub his hands together whenever he got excited about a pending deal that he was about to close. He was totally unaware of this subconscious habit. Any time I wanted him to get excited about a new project, I rubbed my hands together just like he would and my action triggered him to do it too, making him very excited about working on the project.

Finally, you can also create an anchor for yourself to help you get into an advantageous emotional state. If you are about to attend an important interview or negotiation and really want to jump to a more energetic state, select a body movement that inspires you to get excited, such as snapping your fingers. Snap your fingers many times while imagining that feeling of excitement. This will create the anchor. Just before you enter the meeting, snap your finger several times and feel the excitement rise within you.

74

Can you think of a behaviour that seems to come out of nowhere and totally takes control of your mind, your emotions and your actions? Can you figure out if there is an anchor that triggers this response?

Take a moment to list a couple of these types of behaviours and the circumstances behind their formation.

Behaviour 1. How do you think it was formed? Is there an anchor?

Behaviour 2. How do you think it was formed? Is there an anchor?

CHAPTER SIX

Body Dynamics

"There is a crack in everything. That's how the light gets in." – Leonard Cohen

Any discussion about resilience must include a discussion on how your body is an essential piece of the puzzle. I am using the term **'body dynamics' to refer to the many constant affects, changes and shifts that are happening in our body, moment by moment, in relation to our thoughts and emotions.**

The Cambridge English Dictionary defines the word dynamic as ... 'forces or processes that produce change inside a group or system.' There are many body-based tools such deep breathing and movement (e.g. yoga) that cause change in your emotional and mental state. In this chapter we will engage in a thorough exploration of a number of these tools, as well as go over the latest research in mind-body science.

More and more, we see the power of the mind-body connection being used in a variety of tools and therapies that you can take advantage of to maintain your mental and emotional equilibrium. There are many research studies that substantiate the indelible link between our body and our mental health and emotions. A number of the interventions I have used with clients are related to modalities that use both the body and the mind to enable healing and emotional clearing.

The Gut-Brain

One study from Harvard Medical School's online magazine Healthbeat discusses research which shows that **the brain and the gastrointestinal system are closely connected**. Essentially, it is clear that our gastrointestinal tract is sensitive to emotion. Feelings such as anger, anxiety, depression, excitement — all of these feelings (and others) can trigger symptoms in the gut. The term **'gut-brain'** is being used to label this vital connection. You may have heard the phrase 'I had a gut feeling", which typically refers to following your intuition. However, evidence substantiated in many studies conclude that you should also be paying attention to the close connection between your emotional state and your gut.

In the absence of physical causes, doctors are now considering the role of stress and your emotions in finding remedies for digestive ailments. It is increasingly clear that psychological factors influence the physiology of the gut, such as affecting the contractions of the gut lining.

In Healthbeat, researchers review how "13 studies showed that patients who tried psychologically-based approaches had greater improvement in their digestive and intestinal symptoms compared with patients who received only conventional medical treatment." Symptoms such as heartburn and abdominal cramps were alleviated.

Researchers of the gut-brain connection have also reported that **controlling the diverse bacterial population in the gut (know at the microbiome) may help improve mental health** symptoms. Essentially, the overgrowth of 'bad bacteria' can not only reduce the diversity of the 'good bacteria' necessary for good gut health, but also cause inflammation that affects many other biological systems, including the brain. "This system of connections and communication between the gastrointestinal tract and the brain is referred to as the *gut-brain axis*." Some researchers speculate that infections occurring in early life could negatively affect the mucosal membrane in the GI tract, disrupting the gut-brain axis, and interfering with normal brain development. The mucosal membrane can also be altered in other ways, such as through poor diet choices, radiation treatment, antibiotic use, and chemotherapy (https://www.psycom.net)".

Scientists call the gut brain the *enteric nervous system* (ENS). The enteric nervous system is made up of more than 100 million nerve cells that line your gastrointestinal tract starting from the esophagus to rectum. In addition to controlling our digestion through the release of enzymes (and much more), the ENS, also called the second brain, communicates back and forth – through hormones and neurotransmitters – with our brain and appears to trigger mood changes due to irritation in the gastrointestinal system, which sends signals to the central nervous system (CNS).

Jay Pasricha, M.D., director of the Johns Hopkins Center for Neurogastroenterology, states that a "higher-than-normal percentage of people with irritable bowel syndrome and functional bowel problems develop depression and anxiety." This is significant, since up to 30 to 40 percent of the population will experience functional bowel problems at some point in life. As discussed earlier, the **chemical messages** that pass between the gut and the brain can be affected by the bacteria, viruses and fungi that live in the gut (i.e. the microbiome) since the microbiome can be made up of helpful or harmful bacteria, viruses, and fungi. Keeping the right balance of these microbes in the microbiome is vital for both mental and physical health.

Think of how many times we hear about people who engage in "emotional eating" to help suppress stress and anxiety; as you can see, the gut-brain is playing a central part in this process. Remedies that work on both ENS and CNS systems will be very effective in helping with both the physical and psychological symptoms of IBS, such as medication for the gastrointestinal system coupled with the use of tools such as hypnotherapy and cognitive behavioural therapy for the mind. Some doctors are now prescribing antidepressants for IBS to help calm certain symptoms by acting on the nerve cells in the gut.

This is a good time to mention that along with the biochemical and microbiome connection, a physical connection exists between the gut and the brain via the vagus nerve. This nerve controls messages to gut, heart, lungs and other vital organs in the body and has a direct connection with the brain. The importance of the **vagus nerve** will be discussed in-depth in the Emotional Agility chapter, but in the meantime here's a quick overview:

The vagus nerve is the 10th cranial nerve, which plays a key role in dampening your body's 'stress response' in that it aids in counteracting the stress response when you exhale. The vagus nerve interfaces with the parasympathetic nervous system and controls the heart, lungs and digestive tract. So when you do a long and slow exhale (longer than the inhale) the vagus nerves regulates the heart by slowing down your heart rate and lowering blood pressure.

This may be an overly simplistic way to sum up what we know about the gut and brain connection, but it would seem that **a healthy gut can contribute to a healthy brain**.

How do you keep a healthy gut?

Get a check-up from a specialist who can test what is going on in your digestive system to examine the balance of the microbiome. Many clients have found that consuming prebiotics foods (such as garlic, onions, artichokes, leeks, cabbage, asparagus, legumes and oats) and probiotics foods and supplements (which contain live bacteria found in yogurt, kefir, cottage cheese, fresh sauerkraut and apple cider vinegar) is helpful in achieving a balanced microbiome. I usually buy yogurt with live bacteria such as Bifidobacterium and Lactobacillus, which are some of the most common good bacteria.

Also, generally balancing your diet by eating more alkalizing foods vs acidifying foods can make a huge difference in keeping your pH balance in the right range. This is easier said than done, since so much of the food that is easily available is more acidic than alkaline. If you do an Internet search for "acidic vs alkaline foods" you will see many lists that can help you in your food planning. Generally processed foods, excessive sugar (this feeds the natural yeast commonly found in your gut's microbiome), high meat protein diets, fish, alcohol and some dairy products are processed and acid-forming foods.

Excess acid in your stomach and intestines (known as acidosis) has been associated with an overproduction of yeast, which can have negative health consequences, as discussed below. Generally, foods such as fruits, nuts, lemon, legumes and vegetables are alkaline forming-foods.

Something else to think about in keeping a healthy gut is that antibiotics don't discriminate in which bacteria they kill. Antibiotics kill both bad bacteria and unfortunately also the good bacteria that keeps your gut working properly. So, whenever I take a dose of antibiotics, I usually follow-up with a regime of extra probiotics and foods that support a healthy gut microbiome.

If you have a chronic upset stomach, it is vital that you see a doctor or a specialist called a gastroenterologist who can give you a specific diagnosis of the issue.

As I write about the gut-brain I am reminded of a case involving a woman (let's call her Jane), who consulted with me to work through her lack of energy and self-motivation. As it turns out, we uncovered a surprising cause – systemic yeast was an essential part of her problem. In our first session, Jane described a feeling deep sadness; she had no desire to take on anything new at work. These emotional symptoms seemed to be paired with feeling foggy headed, sensitivity to certain smells, insomnia, fatigue, muscle aches and pains, being constantly itchy all over, yeast infections, persistent indigestion, heartburn and regular near-weekly migraines.

As she described her symptoms, I had a hunch about what might be going on due to previous experiences with similar cases. Based on my hunch, I encouraged her to get a pH test (urine), urinalysis and other recommended examinations from her doctor. She then asked her doctor for these tests as part of a checkup. Her blood test came back with a pH level of 5.0, which meant she was acidic.

My suspicion was correct. Jane's bodily acidity, considered acidosis, was likely contributing to her lethargy, nausea, headaches and other symptoms.

The acidity or alkalinity of any solution, blood included, is indicated on the pH scale. Blood is normally slightly basic/alkaline, with a normal pH range of 7.35 to 7.45. Usually the body maintains the pH of blood close to 7.40. A person who has a blood pH below 7.35 is considered to be in acidosis (actually, "physiological acidosis," because blood is not truly acidic until its pH drops below 7). The body has a lot of processes, acid-base homeostasis, to ensure blood pH doesn't change too much outside the normal range.

Over 20 years ago, I learned about the health challenges that our bodies suffer when acidic levels are too high from a book called The Yeast Connection, by William G. Crook. When your body is acidic, it can be a perfect breeding ground for excessive Candida Albicans / yeast growth and other unhealthy microbes.

Systemic yeast growth throughout the body (not just a yeast infection), comes with a long list of symptoms including the ones Jane had. Yeast is naturally found in the body and is helpful in balanced amounts, but toxins from the waste products of large number of yeasts that colonize the mucous membranes in the body will weaken the immune system.

Now Jane knew what she needed to tackle on her path to wellness. So she set out to alkalize her body with a new diet regime of tons of greens (broccoli and spinach), lots of lemon and water, probiotics and she reduced her sugar intake and cut back on acidic foods such as coffee, meat and dairy.

We also worked on releasing years of pent-up negative feelings, as well as realignment with values and life goals. In about 3 months she began to see the physical and emotional benefits of the process. She had a few mild headaches but didn't get another migraine, her indigestion was getting better, and she felt less tired. Emotionally she felt less sad and was excited to take on a new project at work. For Jane, the combination of cleansing the body, repairing the gut, as well as therapies to deal with her emotional state, brought her back to a state of well-being.

Using your body to change your state of mind and emotion

In 2001 I completed my training in Neuro-Linguistic Psychology. During the training, we used an interesting technique to dramatically show how working with our bodies can help us break patterns of negative thinking and emotional upset. We were asked to imagine ourselves thinking that 'life sucks,' then to stand up and act it out. The whole group stood up with heads held down, shrugged shoulders, eyes downcast and sad faces. Then we were asked to hold our heads up and look up to the ceiling with a big smile, and then turn to the person beside us and say 'life sucks.' As you can imagine, we all broke out into laughter – it seemed ridiculous to be smiling and laughing while saying 'life sucks.' Mismatching of the body's expressions and the thoughts you are having is a great way to 'interrupt-the-pattern' of automatic reactions.

If you consistently focus on the worst case scenario, your whole nervous system produces responses related to being in a constant state of fear. Your mind, body and emotions will produce timid and fearful behaviours which will cause you to have poor results. This becomes a self-fulfilling belief, since the poor results confirm that you were right to be fearful and that you weren't going to be successful. Over time, the constant validation of your negative mindset and feelings create automatic reactions with the associated physical behaviours and how you hold and use your body.

You can change the emotional state you are in by changing behaviour and physical actions. In other words, you can change your state of mind by changing how your body reacts through new actions and behaviours that are incongruent with the emotions or thoughts you are having. This means you should shift your posture, hold your head up, force a smile, stretch your arms out, speed up your movements, stand up if you normally sit down, be quiet if you are normally loud, hold your body differently and expand your bodily movements rather than shrink back.

Social psychologist and Harvard professor Amy Cuddy has shown through research that adopting **a "power pose"** associated with dominance and power, such as standing with your hands on your hips and holding your head up like Wonder Woman for just 2 minutes, can significantly lower the level of the stress hormone cortisol in our cells and increase the level of testosterone (which produces a feeling of power). People who adopted this power posing method also reported an increased appetite for risk and better performance in job interviews.

Moving the body through activities such as stretching, dance, yoga and other physical activities not only burns off excess pent-up energy, but is now seen to stimulate the brain in ways where new pathways are formed that help your nervous system to learn the distinction between moments of muscle tension and relaxation.

I use a guided process of progressive muscle relaxation with clients, where they tense and release various muscles in the body. Working from head to toe, the client learns to identity areas of tension by experiencing the different sensations in the body when muscles are tense compared to when the muscles are relaxed. Then I instruct the client to focus their inhaling breath toward the area of tension

84

(especially jaw, neck, shoulders, back, legs), imagining the breath flooding that part of the body, and then to exhale and release. Sometimes we add movement or stretching such as raising their shoulders on the inhale and dropping the shoulders on the exhale.

Using the power of breath to relax the body and calm the nervous system

It has long been known that deep breathing is one of the most powerful techniques for relaxing the body and calming the nervous system. Deep breathing is an active part of all forms of meditation and Mindfulness practices.

Breathing can trigger your natural **relaxation response** especially when you follow a pattern of conscious breaths, such as breathing in for a count of three and then breathing out for a count of five or six. Repeating this pattern for several minutes will bring on a natural feeling of relaxation.

The term "relaxation response" is a well-documented physiological process that was introduced in 1975 in a book called The Relaxation Response by Dr. Herbert Benson and Miriam Z. Klipper. In the late sixties, Harvard Medical School associate professor of medicine Herbert Benson studied Yogis who practiced **Transcendental Meditation (TM),** a 15 to 20 minute silent mantra/sound meditation where you sit silently, with your eyes closed, in meditation while repeating the mantra/sound in your mind to see what beneficial results this form of meditation had on the mind and body.

Those who practiced TM claimed to be able to reduce their blood pressure. After testing them, Dr. Benson found that indeed, people who practiced regular meditation had

85

lower stress levels, reduced blood pressure levels, maintained resting heart rates and had an overall increase in their wellbeing.

The relaxation response is essentially the opposite of the fight-and-flight response and it reduces the physical effects of stress. When we are under stress, our **sympathetic nervous system** creates a cascade of physiological responses such as increases in your metabolism, blood pressure, heart and breathing rate and dilation of your pupils. A cocktail of stress hormones including epinephrine and norepinephrine are released into the bloodstream. Frequent firing of this stress response can cause a variety of stress-related health issues such as heart disease, high blood pressure, and gastrointestinal discomfort. The Relaxation Response turns off this fight and flight response and helps the body return to pre-stress levels. The relaxation response activates the parasympathetic nervous system which engages the body's resting phase.

There are many ways to elicit the Relaxation Response. These include deep breathing, meditation, yoga, guided visualization, hypnosis, progressive relaxation or simply unplugging from your everyday whirlwind of activity and going for a walk in nature.

Dr. Benson describes a **Relaxation Response technique** in his book, which follows several steps. The steps are summarized below:

1. Sit quietly in a comfortable position and close your eyes.
2. Focus on breathing and deeply relax all your muscles, beginning at your feet and progressing up to your face. Keep them relaxed.

3. Breathe through your nose. As you breathe out, say the word "one" silently to yourself. Continue doing this breathing and silently saying the word 'one' for 10 to 20 minutes.

5. You may open your eyes to check the time, but do not use an alarm. When you finish, sit quietly for 3 minutes, at first with your eyes closed and later with your eyes opened.

The best time to practice the relaxation response technique is in the mornings for 10 to 20 minutes. Practicing this at least once a day can be sufficient to counteract the stress response and bring about a state of generalized relaxation.

Vagal Nerve Breathing Exercise

Another very effective breathing exercise for stimulating the parasympathetic nervous system is the **Vagus Nerve Breathing Exercise**. Earlier I mentioned that the vagus nerve connects with the parasympathetic nervous system and controls the heart, lungs and digestive tract. In the vagus nerve breathing exercise, you do a longer, slower exhale than the inhale, which enhances the relaxation effects of the breath. The inhale speeds up the heart so that the heart can pump oxygen throughout the body (a slight activation of the sympathetic nervous system) and the exhale relaxes the body due to a slight activation of the parasympathetic nervous system.

The basic formula for the Vagus Nerve Breathing technique is to breathe in for a count of 3 to 4 and exhale slowly for a count of 6 to 8. The idea is to stimulate the parasympathetic system with the extended out-breath. Do this practice several times per day for at least 2 minutes, for a cycle of 5 to 10 breaths.

When breathing, remember to take a longer and slower exhale than the inhale. This will allow the vagus nerves to slow down your heart rate and lower your blood pressure. We will cover other breathing techniques such sighing and diaphragmatic breathing (also called the belly breath) in the Mindfulness chapter.

Touch Therapies

All the tools and techniques we have discussed so far provide the means to reset the **autonomic nervous system** (this is made up of the sympathetic and parasympathetic nervous system and controls the bodily functions that are not consciously directed, such as breathing, the heartbeat, and digestive processes) and retrain your brain to reinforce the natural resilience that is built into the mind-body connection.

Touch sensation is yet another way to connect with our bodies calming centres. There are many forms of touch therapies such as Therapeutic Touch (non-contact therapeutic touch where the practitioner holds their hands above parts of their client's body), Emotional Freedom Therapy (based on tapping acupressure points on the face and the body) and many more. In this section, I am covering simple touch therapies which you can do on your own without any special training.

Touch can elicit relaxation, restores cellular communication and causes the release of Oxytocin in the body. Oxytocin is a hormone generated by the pituitary gland, that has a number of positive functions in the body. The two I want to highlight here are its role in social bonding and in the reduction of stress. The most recent research shows oxytocin as having an important role in social behaviours such as mother-infant bonding, trust, and safety. It is sometimes called the 'cuddle chemical' or 'love hormone' because it is released when we snuggle or bond socially. According to a study in 2009 in the Journal of Hormones and Behavior, playing with a pet can cause oxytocin to be released as well. Oxytocin can be released by sensory stimulation, for example by touch. Gentle touch can produce these very positive feelings of connection which are essential for a sense of wellbeing.

Oxytocin also has anti-stress effects on the body by reducing cortisol in the bloodstream. Cortisol is the hormone that is secreted when you are stressed. Overall, oxytocin helps you reduce stress symptoms through the reduction of blood pressure and increase in your pain threshold. This 'love hormone' stimulates the desire for positive social interactions which is essential for promoting healing and well-being.

Here is a simple **touch and visualization exercise** that I have used successfully for myself and with clients, to help bring about a sense of calm, comfort and connection:

1. *Place both hands on your chest, with your right hand slightly touching the centre and toward the left-side of your chest (over the heart) and the left hand crossed on top of the right hand and slightly on the right-side of your chest.*
2. *As you inhale, notice the breath filling up your chest and lower abdomen, and let your hand and fingers feel your chest rising.*
3. *Exhale slowly, taking twice as long as the inhale. Counting the inhale and exhale is a great way to keep track of the length of each breath.*
4. *Repeat steps 2 and 3 for a total of 5 breaths.*

5. *As you continue breathing, imagine a time when you felt most <u>calm</u>, remembering how you felt, what you saw, and what you heard.*
6. *Next, think about a time when you felt most <u>safe</u>, remembering how you felt, what you saw, and what you heard.*
7. *Finally, think about a time when you felt most <u>loved</u>, remembering how you felt, what you saw, and what you heard.*

The more that you practice this technique, the more it will become anchored in your subconscious as a powerful resource that you can use any time to bring about these positive feelings. Daily practice will strengthen the neural circuits, training your brain to be resilient and create new responses to challenging situations. The self-soothing touch will also stimulate the release of oxytocin, bathing every cell in your body with its calming influence.

Somatic Healing

The word 'soma' is a Greek word which translates generally to 'the living body.' The theory behind somatic therapy is that traumatic symptoms are the effects of an unstable autonomic nervous system (ANS) in that the trauma disrupts the normal workings of the ANS. All emotions have a physical aspect and **somatization** is the term used for the physical expressions of stress and emotions that become trapped in the body. In other words, **somatization** is when our bodies hold onto past traumas and is expressed in body through our body language, posture and other physical symptoms such as chronic pain, digestive issues, hormonal imbalance and possible immune deficiencies. There can also be residual psychological conditions such as anxiety and depression.

I worked with a client who suffered from irritable bowel syndrome (IBS). When we first met, he described how he would be fine for weeks and suddenly, with no apparent reason, he would get indigestion, diarrhea and other gastrointestinal discomfort. He felt there was some emotional trigger, but he was unable to pinpoint what it could be. After some discussion, he remembered an incident back in high school where he had felt put on the spot because he had to make a crucial catch to help his team win the game.

As he ran forward to catch the ball, he noticed an opposing player charging toward him. He froze up for just a moment, but it was long enough for the player to head-butt him straight in the abdomen, and down to the ground he fell. He didn't remember the physical pain from being attacked so aggressively, he only remembered being embarrassed and angry that he had failed his team. As he recounted the story, he began to feel a pain in his stomach and abdomen. I asked him to describe the pain, and he told me it was like being punched and he felt winded. I asked him to focus on taking a deep breath and slowly exhaling, and the intensity of the pain reduced. He felt much better by the end of the session.

A few days later, he called to tell me his revelation – he had realized that his body would act up whenever he had a big presentation or report to make for his team where he feared he might fail or disappoint. He said "it was like re-living that moment" – the traumatic moment from his schooldays where he had originally paired failure with physical pain.

Although we also worked on other issues, the main outcome of our counselling sessions was that he was able to feel a decrease in his IBS symptoms as he practiced confronting painful memories by re-experiencing the sensations of that day back in high school while describing them. This process helped him to integrate the experience over time.

When an emotional experience gets separated from the cognitive processing of that experience, such as through trauma or sudden shock, it often results in a lack of integration and trapped sensations in the body that can go unexplained for many years. The integration process my client experienced is a therapeutic approach which combines the use of the emotional centres of the brain with the executive functions of the brain to create a synthesis of physical memory (somatization) with emotions, which can lead to healing and a state of well-being.

Another case of somatization involved a woman who came to see me about chronic pain in her side. She had been to a number of medical specialists in an attempt to find out what might be causing the pain. They found no disease or physical cause. She thought hypnotherapy might be helpful, so she booked a session with me.

After getting a brief overview of personal history, I performed the hypnotic induction and, through a guided visualization process, directed her to imagine that she was looking at the pain. I asked her, Did it have a shape, a colour, a texture, was it hot or cold? We used this abstract process to describe the pain. She was able to describe the colour, texture, shape, and so on. Once she could describe it and envision it, I asked her if she was ready to let it go. She said yes, and I guided her to imagine the pain dissolving.

As soon as she opened her eyes and emerged out of hypnosis, she remarked, "It's gone, the pain is gone." She also remembered a past trauma that she experienced while growing up. She said it was as if the memories were trapped in her body and the chronic pain marked the spot. The pain did not come back after that first session, and her focus shifted to processing the negative memories.

Somatic psychotherapy is a mind-body therapy and is one of a number of body-oriented approaches to healing trauma. In their 1997 book "Walking The Tiger: Healing Trauma," psychotherapists Peter A. Levine and Ann Frederick describe somatic psychotherapy as a means to relieve symptoms of mental and physical trauma-related health issues focused on the client's body sensations. Levine has gone on to create a body-oriented approach to healing trauma and stress disorders based upon his 45 years of clinical application. This process involves helping those who are considered to be stuck in the fight, flight and freeze responses with clinical methods to get them past physiological symptoms.

In Levine's healing process, the practitioner works to create completion of the 'freeze' protective motor responses and to release trapped energy and tension in the body. This in turn serves to remedy the root cause of the trauma symptoms. Clients are taught to develop increased tolerance of uncomfortable physical sensations and suppressed emotions. The premise of this therapy is to work with the 'body memory' of the trauma as an essential aspect to completing the healing. Levine believes that an overwhelming response to a perceived threat has caused an imbalance in the nervous system which results in trapped and unresolved energy in the body. This stuck energy that was preparing you for fight and flight builds up and needs to be discharged (typically through shaking and trembling), otherwise the body may still perceive that it is under threat.

Nineteen years ago I was running a retreat workshop for women called 'Personal Mastery – Reclaiming The Warrior Within' when I encountered a participant (I will call her Barbara) who experienced a big release of energy. I was guiding participants through a guided visualization technique which involved reviewing their past timelines and then allowing their subconscious to drift to a memory that they were ready to re-witness, reframe, and from which to release any pent up feelings.

Just as I asked the group to open their eyes, I noticed Barbara's whole body was shaking and trembling. Her breathing was very shallow. I asked everyone to take a stretch break and immediately walked over to Barbara and asked her to fully open her eyes, focus on her breath and exhale slowly. She began breathing deeply as she continued to shake and tremble. Her body became calmer after several deep breaths and the trembling reduced, so I asked her to walk with me and guided her out of the room.

We were in a beautiful resort setting with many tree-lined paths, so we headed for the one closest to the conference room. When we stepped onto the path, she said "I feel like running," so we ran together for about 5 minutes, then she stopped and sat down on the grass beside the pathway.

"Holy s***," Barbara exclaimed. "That was some experience!" She wasn't trembling or shaking anymore and her breathing was back to normal. "I feel so different, everything looks so much brighter now, and my foggy head and tightness in my neck and shoulders is all gone."

I noticed the muscles in her face had softened and she seemed much more relaxed. I asked her if she wanted to talk more about what she experienced, and she said, "It was amazing, I literally felt my body letting go of all these feelings I had about a bad time in my life."

I told her that I was so happy for her transformation. We never talked about anything else. For the rest of the retreat Barbara had a big smile on her face, as if she had figured out some big secret of the universe. She spent a good part of her time at the retreat supporting others, and the effects of that day lasted well beyond that week. Several years later she told me that that day changed her life in such as positive way for good.

Biofeedback: A tool to control involuntary body functions to manage stress, anxiety and pain

Biofeedback is a technique you can use to learn to control some of your body's functions in order to treat physical issues such as your heart rate, migraines, blood pressure and chronic pain. It is also used to teach individuals how to manage stress by teaching them relaxation techniques. There is also extensive research which illustrates that biofeedback therapy can be effective in treating anxiety disorders. During biofeedback, you are connected to devices with electrical sensors that help you receive information about your body, and you are taught how to properly respond to your anxiety.

During a **biofeedback** session, electrodes are attached to your skin. Finger sensors or a headband are often used. These electrodes/sensors send signals to a monitor, which displays a sound, a light, or an image that represents your heart and breathing rate, blood pressure, skin temperature, sweating, or muscle activity. These functions are typically controlled involuntarily by your nervous system but with biofeedback, you can learn to gain some control over these normally involuntary functions as a way to monitor and intentionally control them.

When you are under stress, the biofeedback device will typically show a faster heart rate, tightened muscles tension, rising blood pressure and quickened breathing. The biofeedback therapist would then guide you into a variety of relaxation methods in which you direct mindful attention to a specific body function such as your heart rate to learn to slow it down. As you become aware of what is happening inside you, you use one of the relaxation techniques to affect your body's function. As you begin to slow your heart rate, lower your blood pressure, and ease muscle tension, you'll get instant feedback on the biofeedback equipment screen. Over time, you learn to control these functions on your own, without the equipment.

Some of the relaxation techniques can include deep breathing, Mindful meditation, guided visualization intended to have you focus your mind on an image to promote relaxation and progressive muscle relaxation (contracting and relaxing the muscles from head to toe).

In addition to chronic pain, managing anxiety is one of the most common uses of biofeedback. Biofeedback will help you become more aware of your body's typical reactions when you are stressed and anxious. As your awareness grows, you begin to learn how to control those reactions with biofeedback equipment, and with practice you eventually gain the benefit of being able to control your anxiety without the use of any devices. The power comes from having the process become an ingrained natural resource that is available to you any time you need it.

I have had friends who were skeptical about biofeedback. "Does it really work?" they would ask. Yes, I'd tell them, I have experienced it myself. I have successfully decreased my heart rate and blood pressure (bp) by using biofeedback. I use a blood pressure monitor to take a reading before and after using biofeedback to measure the change in bp level.

Recently, my good friend Don gifted me a device called the 'Muse Headband.' This device is designed to help us learn to relax the mind. You put on a headband which touches your forehead and behind your ears, and then you connect the Muse to the App (available for iPhone and Android) on your phone or tablet. The Muse is a research-based EEG device which senses your brain activity and translates it into sounds of nature to help you learn to stay calm and focused on mindful meditation.

I use the Muse with my iPad mini. When I first put on the Muse, I heard a stormy weather sound through my iPad headphones. As I focused on breathing deeply and going into a deep meditation, there was a more peaceful, quieter weather sound. The Muse provided real-time feedback on how well my meditation was going. The more I used it, the quicker I was able to establish a calm state. On the Muse website they discuss documented research about the benefits of meditation which produces brain structure changes including increased grey matter density, reduced thinning of the prefrontal cortex (the centre of the brain's executive functions) and decreased amygdala activity which is associated with the stress response.

You can **learn biofeedback** with a trained specialist at a biofeedback centre, or through computer programs that connect the biofeedback sensor to your own computer, or with a device like the Muse Headband.

This chapter on Body Dynamics illustrates the natural healing power of the mind-body relationship and the many body-based tools and therapies that are available to you to bring about healing of the mind, body and emotions. When we nurture and strengthen the mind-body connection we enhance our resilience and our ability to access internal resources that help us to interrupt negative patterns of thinking and emotionality and to reset our nervous system to a calmer state.

Learning in Action - Body Dynamics

Use the following table to plan, set timelines and track your progress on each of the components, taking advantage of the mind-body connection.

Component / Tools / Process	Action Plan – In the next 90 days when will you do it? Track your notes in the column below.
Gut Health – Do you have a balanced microbiome?	
Shift your diet to be more alkaline rather than acidic to support gut health	
Use your body to shift your mindset by interrupting patterns of reaction, thinking and emotions.	
Do a 2 minute **Power Pose** to reduce the stress hormone levels	
Find a **Biofeedback** centre in your area by doing an Internet search	
Practice the **Relaxation Response Technique** for 10 to 20 minutes each day	
Vagal Nerve breathing exercise – breath in for a count of 4 and slowly exhale for a count of 8.	
Somatic Healing – how can this help you?	

CHAPTER SEVEN

Mindfulness

"The secret of health for both mind and body is not to mourn for the past, worry about the future, or anticipate troubles, but to live in the present moment wisely and earnestly." – Buddha

The most common practice in Mindfulness is meditation. Mindfulness originated from an ancient Buddhist meditation technique, but has since evolved into a range of secular therapies and courses which are not related to any particular religion or spiritual practice. Mindfulness programs focus on becoming aware of the present moment and paying attention to feelings and thoughts as they come and go.

Mindful meditation as a tool is used to combat the effects of stress and anxiety, and its benefits have been supported by numerous research studies for more than a decade. It has been extensively used for stress management as part of a program called the Mindfulness-Based Stress Reduction (MBSR), which was developed by Jon Kabat-Zinn from the University of Massachusetts Medical School. Dr. Kabat-Zinn's definition of Mindfulness is *"paying attention, on purpose, in the present moment, non-judgmentally."* Kabat-Zinn conducted an 8 week program in MBSR at the University's Stress Reduction Clinic and found that practicing mindful meditation brought about beneficial improvements in both the physical and psychological symptoms of participants taking part in the study. Participants had reduction in their stress and overall health improvements.

Professor Mark Williams of the Oxford Mindfulness Centre has conducted a number of research programs on Mindfulness using MRI brain scans, which showed a marked difference in the brains of people who practiced mindful meditation. After an eight-week course of mindfulness practice, the brain's "fight or flight" center, the amygdala, appears to shrink. This primal region of the brain, associated with fear and emotion, is involved in the initiation of the body's stress response. When the amygdala shrinks, your fear response is dampened down, and the pre-frontal cortex – associated with higher order brain functions such as awareness, concentration and decision-making – becomes thicker.

Mindfulness practices are processes designed to bring one's attention to experiences occurring in the present moment. So why is it beneficial to stay in the here and now? Studies in mindfulness show that constant rumination and worrying about things we cannot change or that are out of our control can contribute to the onset of a variety of stress-based disorders such as anxiety. Mindfulness-based interventions are seen to significantly reduce rumination. Performing a mindful practice keeps us from dwelling on the past or trying to anticipate what will happen in the future.

When you meditate, you are paying attention to whatever you have chosen as an area of focus: you become aware of your breathing, thoughts, body sensations and emotions. Meditation can help you to discover patterns in your thinking as well as notice the impact these patterns have on your emotions, choices and decisions.

In addition to meditation, there are a number of other Mindfulness Practices such as mindful listening, mindful walking and mindful eating. When you perform any of these mindful activities, you are singularly focused on what you are doing in that moment. You have complete awareness of your thoughts, emotions and physical sensations and purposely keep your mind from wandering to unrelated thoughts. For example, in mindful eating you pay attention to each piece of food you put in your mouth, and fully engage with your senses – the colour, taste, texture and smell of what is on your plate.

As you embark on your mindfulness practice, you are encouraged to imagine that you are seeing aspects of yourself and others with fresh eyes, as if for the first time. This will allow you to see things as they are and not as you expect them to be.

Catch yourself before you start projecting what you expect to see based on any preconceived notions you may have; instead, aim to rekindle your curiosity, which seeks new perspectives.

Mindfulness brings greater awareness. Awareness makes you more conscious of your experience in the 'moment.' Not allowing yourself to get trapped in the past or preoccupied with the future, but remaining grounded in the present moment.

The present moment is being aware of the *here* and *now* of your experience, seeing it *as it is* without trying to attribute any particular meaning or reacting to the experience. It feels natural to react to the thoughts that arise within you. Many of your reactions are automatic and reflexive, and often not something you consciously choose. Mindfulness allows you to *choose the response* to the experience you are having in the present moment, rather than having a conditioned, *automatic reaction*, something we discussed in the chapter on Mental Fortitude.

The Breath

The breath is the focal point for your attention when you engage in Mindfulness Practices. Focusing your attention on the sensation of breathing provides a means to bring yourself into the present moment and gain awareness of your thoughts, emotions and body sensations. The phrase "belly breath" is used because you are encouraged to take deep breaths all the way down to your lower abdomen. A technical term for this form of breathing is called *diaphragmatic breathing.*

The diaphragm is the most efficient muscle for breathing. It is a large, dome-shaped muscle located at the base of the lungs. Your abdominal muscles help move the diaphragm and give you more power to empty your lungs when you exhale.

To practice diaphragmatic breathing, place one hand just below your rib cage. As you inhale, breathe in slowly through your nose so that your stomach moves out against your hand; it should balloon outwards as you fill up with air. As you exhale, tighten your stomach muscles, letting them push inward as you exhale – this results in a more complete exhalation.

During a guided Mindfulness Practice, the facilitator will often tell you to bring your attention back to your breath if you feel distracted in any way. This type of breathing will also strengthen your diaphragm muscle and enhance deeper breathing. Most people going about their everyday activities tend to have shallower breathing, where they inhale only into their chest. Focusing on breathing into your diaphragm creates a richer oxygenation of your body.

Three Pillars of Mindfulness

The three key pillars of mindfulness are Intention, Attention and Attitude. These aspects of mindfulness come together to help you bring on a state of mindful awareness. **Intention** is what you hope to get from your mindfulness practice, such as stress reduction, relaxation, pain management, a greater sense of peace and increased emotional regulation.

Attention is about paying attention to an inner or outer experience. You build your mindful attention through meditation. Attention another way of saying "focused awareness." Mindfulness training helps you to develop your ability to pay attention and become more aware wherever and whenever you want. Paying attention to your breathing serves as the first object of attention. This practice will bring your awareness to the present moment. Your intention is not to prevent thinking, but to allow thinking to pass through your mind without resistance.

Finally, **Attitude** is your ability to choose and maintain a certain value or principle in your mind, which is one of the key principles in MBSR Mindfulness. Mindfulness practice encourages that you hold higher principles in your heart, such as empathy for yourself and others, patience, acceptance, letting go of negative emotions, and being non-judgmental.

Non-Judgmental

Being non-judgmental requires paying attention to your thoughts, moment by moment, without getting fixated upon your own personal preferences, likes and dislikes, opinions or motives. We are constantly judging and interpreting our experiences. Can you suspend the "judger" in yourself during your mindfulness practice? Are you holding on to the "positive" feelings and avoiding the "negative" ones? Can you interrupt this automatic habit of categorizing and labeling behaviours?

Become a neutral observer and suspend the desire to interpret and draw conclusions from what you are experiencing. One way to break this pattern of behaviour is not to stop the thoughts that might come to you during your practice – just allow them to float in and out of your mind as you bring your attention back to your in-breath and out-breath.

Exercise: What percentage of your day do you spend on making judgements? Less than 50% or more than 50%? Although we cannot suspend judgement totally, we can aim to reduce it when we find ourselves becoming too self-critical. Suspending judgment will allow us to minimize self-criticism and be more present in the moment.

Patience

Mindfulness asks that we nurture a patient mind by allowing things to unfold in their own time. It may take you longer to achieve a quiet mind; remember not to compare your progress with the progress of others. Your mind has a way of *wandering* from the present and *wondering* about what's going on around us. Your mind can have anxiety-producing thoughts that keep you stuck ruminating about the past or trying to anticipate the future.

When you are practicing mindfulness, don't resist the thoughts that might come up, and don't hold onto them. Just notice these thoughts floating through your mind and allow yourself to experience a sense of calm and well-being.

As you practice mindfulness, give yourself permission to feel empathy for yourself and allow any guilt, bitterness or resentments to dissolve. Also grant the same for others as you contemplate forgiveness and letting go of past hurts. Self-acceptance comes when you stop judging aspects of yourself, which gets easier as you develop self-empathy.

Mindful Practices

When you start your Mindfulness Practice, it can be difficult to sit in meditation for long periods of time. I recommend that you start your practice with small doses, such as a one minute tool, then building up to a 20-min practice. Most people need around 15 to 20 minutes before their mind begins to settle, so I recommend that your target goal is meditate for at least 20 minutes in a sitting. Kabat-Zinn recommends 45 minutes per session six days/week.

When you build up to a 20 minute practice, you mind will grow calmer and you will begin to gain both psychological and physiological benefits. The schematic at the end of this chapter shows how you can expand your practice over time – starting with a shorter 1 minute practice that you can do several times per day, such as Take Five, and building up to a 3-minute practice and finally longer practices such as Body Scan, Mindful Listening and Mindful Walking. You can find the scripts for several of these practices in the next few pages.

It is important to get a general understanding of meditation so that when you start doing it you will know what to expect, which will put your mind at ease. The basic steps typically included in a Mindful meditation script are outlined as follows:

1. *Sit on a chair and notice the feeling of the chair against your back (alternatively you can sit cross-legged on the floor and notice the floor beneath you).*
2. *Focus on the soles of your feet and notice how it feels.*
3. *Focus on your breathing, on the sensations of air flowing into your nose and out of your mouth, and notice your belly rising with the inhale and falling on the exhale.*
4. *Become aware of any sounds, sensations, and thoughts flowing through your mind.*
5. *Embrace and consider each thought or sensation without judging it as good or bad. If your mind gets distracted, return your focus to your breathing.*

Three Minute Mindfulness Practice (Sitting)

1. Sit in a comfortable position. Allow both soles of your feet to connect to the floor.

2. Rest your hands on your thighs and let your shoulders drop.

3. Gently close your eyes if you feel comfortable doing so OR look for a reference point somewhere on the floor. If you get distracted and your eyes begin to wander around the room, bring them back to this spot.

4. Notice the feeling of your soles against the surface beneath. Notice the feeling of your back against the chair.

5. Feel your spine grow tall against your chair.

6. Take a moment to notice how your body feels.

7. Now bring your attention to the flow of your breath, breathing in and breathing out.

8. You don't need to breathe in a special way because your body knows how to breathe.

9. Simply notice each breath coming into the body as you inhale, and leaving the body as you exhale.

10. If you notice your mind getting caught up in thoughts, concerns, emotions or body sensations, know that this is normal.

11. Notice what is distracting you and gently let it go by redirecting your attention back to the breath.

12. Allow each in-breath to be a new beginning and each out-breath a letting go. When you are ready, slowly bring your attention back to the room, then open your eyes.

This practice helps us to:
1. Be a neutral observer by witnessing our whole experience 2. Narrow our experience by focusing our attention on our breath 3. Expand our awareness to notice more around us

Body Scan (20 – 30 min / sitting or laying down)

Sit comfortably in your chair or lie down on your back. Focus your attention on the soles of your feet.

1. Rest your hands comfortably on your lap or, if you're lying down, next to your body.

2. Gently close your eyes if you feel comfortable doing so OR pick a spot on the floor or wall across from you and fix your gaze.

3. As you inhale, raise your shoulders and allow your shoulders to drop when you exhale.

4. Take a moment to notice how your body feels – there's no right or wrong way to feel, so just allow yourself to experience how it feels right now.

5. With each exhale, allow your body weight to let go and be fully received by the surface beneath you.

6. At the end of your out-breath, allow your awareness to travel through your entire body.

7. As you scan your body from head to toe, allow any sensation to come into your awareness.

8. Stay in the moment and allow yourself to tap into how your body feels in this moment.

9. With your next out-breath focus on the back of your head. What do you notice?

10. If you notice that your mind is caught up in thoughts, concerns, emotions or body sensations, know that this is normal.

11. Now reflect on the sensations in your face, from forehead to chin, and release all tension, allowing all your facial muscles to soften.

12. At the end of the next out-breath, shift your focus on the length of your arm, from your shoulder down to your wrist, allowing the muscles to soften.

13. Think about the palms of your hands, then the back of your hand, then your fingers and nails where it touches the surface beneath.

14. Move your attention to your chest and notice the rising and falling of the chest as you breathe in and out.

15. Allow your attention to move to your stomach. If you notice a sensation of hunger in your stomach, bring your attention back to your breath. With the out-breath, experience the letting go and releasing of tension.

16. Now bring your attention to your hips and allow those muscles to soften and relax.

17. With your next out-breath, bring your attention to your feet, from the soles to the toes.

18. Simply notice any sensation as it arises and remain open to what the body is telling you.

19. Next, bring your attention to the flow of your breath, breathing in and breathing out.

20. Whenever you are ready, count from one to five. On the count of five, bring your attention back into the room.

Mindful Listening (20 min / sitting)

Sit comfortably in your chair. Focus your attention on the soles of your feet.

1. Rest your hands comfortably on your thighs.
2. As you inhale, raise your shoulders and allow your shoulders to drop when you exhale.
3. Gently close your eyes if you feel comfortable doing so OR pick a spot on the floor or wall across from you and fix your gaze.
4. Notice the feeling of your back against the chair and your spine growing tall.
5. Take a moment to notice how your body feels. There's no right or wrong way to feel, so just allow yourself to experience the sensation of how it feels right now.
6. Allow yourself to notice the sounds around you, as your body relaxes even further.
7. Next, bring your attention to the flow of your breath, breathing in and breathing out.
8. You don't need to breathe in a special way because your body knows how to breathe.
9. Simply notice each breath coming into the body as you inhale, and leaving the body as you exhale.
10. If you notice your mind getting caught in thoughts, concerns, emotions or physical sensations, know that this is normal.
11. Notice what is distracting you and gently let it go by redirecting your attention back to the breath.
12. Focus your attention on the experience of hearing and allow sounds to come and go, just like how your breath comes and goes.

13. Move your listening beyond this room and perceive what else you hear.

14. Notice how a sound may appear, linger and disappear as it anchors you in the present moment.

15. Now focus on the most immediate sounds in this room. Allow these sounds to fade as you refocus your attention on your breath.

16. Each inhale is a fresh beginning and each exhale is a letting go. Whenever you are ready, count from one to five. On the count of five, bring your attention back into the room.

10 Practice Tips

1. Be patient with yourself. You may find yourself fidgeting or distracted at first, but this is natural. Refocus by bringing attention back to your breath.

2. Do several Take Fives throughout the day.

3. Commit to at least one 5-Minute Practice per day for a month. Then build up to longer practices such as the body scan and mindful listening.

4. You need discipline to create a sustainable habit, so make it a ritual. I have a specific chair and mat that I use each time I do a Mindful Practice. This creates a psychological anchor.

5. Be gentle with yourself and forgive yourself if you slip up and miss a day; just continue the next day.

6. Team up with a mindfulness buddy and commit to text each other every time you complete a practice.

7. Don't resist what is arising – just allow thoughts, emotions and body sensations to naturally pass, and focus on your breath.

8. Track your progress – each time you complete a practice, jot it down in your smartphone or journal.
9. Take note of your experiences without judgement but with gentleness, curiosity and acknowledgment.
10. Pay attention, on purpose with intention and with an open attitude!

Remember to pay attention to what comes up for you during Mindfulness Practice!
(Table From Mindfulness-Based Cognitive Therapy)

As you begin to build your Mindfulness Practice, I recommend that you track each session in your journal. The table below is a great tool for recording what arises (i.e. what memories, emotions, thoughts or body sensations come up) each time you do a practice.

Situation	Emotions	Body Sensations	Automatic Thoughts (Images)

CHAPTER EIGHT

Personal Mastery

*"Yesterday I was clever, so I wanted to change the world.
Today I am wise, so I am changing myself." – Rumi*

Personal Mastery is the capacity to produce powerful results in any area of your life. When you achieve self-mastery, you gain a profound sense of resilience and joy that comes from a deep-rooted understanding of who you are and what you want out of life. You develop a keen level of self-awareness that conveys insights into your values, beliefs, strengths, weaknesses, and motivations. You begin to understand the reasons why you make the choices you make and act as you do. You proactively and mindfully work to change any thoughts, emotions and behaviours that negatively impact your life when at work or at play.

Personal Mastery means you have Mental Fortitude, Emotional Agility, and have cultivated a strong mind-body connection using the techniques of Body Dynamics. Practicing Personal Mastery encourages individuals to discover more about themselves, teaches them efficient ways to achieve self-control, and enables them to understand and manage variable states of mind and body to create a powerful state of being.

In the Mental Fortitude chapter, you were presented with a values exercise that forms a blueprint through which you can evaluate your personal values, choices and desired goals. In this chapter we will focus on learning ways to build self-awareness, and look at methods to challenge and shift beliefs and behaviours that keep us from building the life we want. Once this self-exploration has been done, we will examine self-identity and how it impacts our self-awareness.

Building self-awareness

Self-awareness is a vital component of emotional intelligence. It gives you the ability to recognize your own feelings, thoughts, internal conflicts and world view. Building your **self-awareness** empowers you with a deeper understanding of how your feelings contribute to your actions. Instead of blaming others and looking at external reasons for what is going wrong in your life, self-awareness provides you the courage to look at what you can do to make a difference for yourself. Self-awareness means that you listen to your internal authority for direction in developing insights into ways to increase personal fulfilment.

There are many ways to build your self-awareness. These include self-reflection, journaling, watching and documenting your thoughts and emotions, noticing habitual things you say and do, and asking a trusted person to tell you how they perceive your behaviour.

One method for building your self-awareness is to *watch* **your thoughts, emotions and reactions** for a few weeks and document them. The biggest challenge to developing self-insight is that most of us analyze our reactions to an experience while we are having the experience. **Reflecting** on the experience is essential, but it's often too difficult to evaluate your emotions rationally while a situation is occurring, particularly in highly-stressful or crisis circumstances.

Stepping back and rewinding the events of the day so that you can see and learn from what happened is a vital aspect of self-reflection. This is the reason why so many self-help books recommend **journaling**. Once you write down your observations, you gain the opportunity to look at your thoughts, emotions and actions in a more objective way. As you write down your experiences, you become a witness to your own behaviour, essentially 'looking' at your thinking process.

Think about how valuable journaling could be when you have conflict with team members, or when you reflect back on an argument with your spouse. We've all had experiences where we have reacted inappropriately toward a colleague or loved one, each accusing the other of doing or saying things that neither of you remember saying or doing. These reactions happen automatically and are usually due to emotional hijack, as discussed in the chapter on Emotional Agility. Rather than just moving on and trying to forget that the conflict happened, take this opportunity to learn something about yourself by *reflecting* on the situation.

When I work with clients, I use a simple table to track and deconstruct the narratives in order to identify patterns in their personal histories. The following table is a sample of the form I use in my practice, and one that you could use to guide your journaling. As a test run, use this form to debrief a situation where you felt that you overreacted. Write your answers in column 2. You can also create a similar chart to reflect on what you observed from the other person with whom you had the altercation. This will help you to perceive how you and the other person may have contributed to the conflict.

Questions to evaluate daily events or specific tough situations	My self-observations
What was I thinking?	
What did I say?	
What did I do (how did I behave)?	
How did I feel?	

When you start to deconstruct what happened in your journal, **you begin to notice your triggers and patterns of reaction**. Russian physiologist Ivan Pavlov, the famous father of classical conditioning, would call it the *stimulus-response cycle*.

As you become aware of your triggers and patterns, it is hard not to notice yourself repeating the cycle. This increasing **awareness gives you an opportunity to catch yourself** at the stimuli stage, offering you a chance to stop before the pattern cascades into a full-blown reaction. The more you pay attention, the more flexibility you will develop in how you **choose** to respond. You can use your body to help you interrupt-the-pattern such as getting up and walking around, or adopting a Power Pose. This involves taking a deep breath, standing tall and holding your head up high with a smile. Stay this way for at least 2 minutes. Then choose how you really want to respond.

Once you have kept notes on your observations for few weeks, read through all the entries and see if any patterns emerge about self-sabotaging thoughts, emotional reactions and behaviours that may interfere with your ability to cope with everyday challenges or add unwanted drama and difficulty with your social or workplace interactions.

Working with beliefs

Another **useful tool for uncovering deeply held beliefs** is to review what you commonly say to yourself about yourself, or what you tell others about you. Your beliefs are personal rules that you create, which either enable or block you from succeeding. Your beliefs and self-talk determine what you perceive and what you don't perceive in the world. In other words, your perceptual filters are defined by your beliefs. Beliefs are like magnets, determining what you see and attract into your life. Having clarity about your beliefs, and specifically overcoming limiting beliefs, helps you to achieve self-mastery.

Our beliefs reveal themselves through thoughts and words. Do you sometimes put yourself down? Do you do it often? What are the self-defeating things you say to yourself? Do you have positive things that you say to yourself to enhance your mood or build your self-esteem?

Many of the habitual things we say to ourselves are a result of the phrases we heard over and over while growing up, which frequently become internalized, subconsciously-held beliefs. As discussed in the chapter on Mental Fortitude, our brains are wired to have a **negativity bias** – a predisposition to pay attention to negative things more than positive things. This means that you are likelier to remember and repeat the negative things that you heard growing up more than the positive things.

I met my client Grace in 2016. She was having a crippling case of low self-esteem and imposter syndrome (she felt that she wasn't qualified and didn't belong in her job), and wanted to find a way to change the 'tapes' in her head. She described this self-talk as tapes that played over and over in her head, telling her that she didn't really know what she was doing. Even though she had successfully made her way up the corporate ladder to become a director for the company where she worked, she was terrified to take the new vice-president position she was offered.

It was the second time in a couple years that senior leaders had offered Grace the new role, and she felt that she couldn't keep saying no because they might start to lose confidence in her. I asked her why she was so convinced that she could not succeed at this new position, since she had been so successful to date.

Grace described how, throughout her childhood, her father frequently told her and her siblings that they were useless and wouldn't amount to anything. On the morning after her boss asked her to meet with him to discuss the promotion, she literally woke up hearing her father's voice in her head. Her fear of the promotion brought her right back to seeing herself as a kid and feeling depressed about her father's berating comments.

I asked her if she still interacted with her father. She said that no, she hadn't because he'd died seven years earlier. I then asked her, "Who is keeping his voice alive in your head?" She gave me a puzzled look and then, after a long moment, she exclaimed, "Oh my goodness, it's me!"

Once the realization sunk in, I asked, "Are you ready to stop repeating those negative things to yourself?" She was quick to respond: "Yes, I want to and I will."

Grace's nonstop repetition of negative statements had become overwhelming. She needed to unbind herself from these harmful thoughts and emotions, and shift her focus to her inner strengths and values. These positive attributes would help her make new choices that were not fear-based, that she found much more fulfilling, and that contributed to her overall personal and professional growth.

We developed a regime of activities to help Grace release the non-empowering habitual thinking that had held her back for so long. This involved challenging the self-defeating thoughts and beliefs that formed the basis of her imposter syndrome. We also worked on getting her unstuck by clearing away the head clutter that was limiting her potential and standing in the way of her success. To do this, we used a combination of hypnosis, positive daily affirmations and self-talk to boost her confidence and self-esteem.

*One of the activities Grace found very helpful was to create an **'accomplishment portfolio'** where she listed everything she was very proud of – all the projects, awards, promotions, awards, certifications, professional development and testimonials from her managers and colleagues, and finally every wonderful thing that was every said about her. Grace put a lot of time and attention in putting together a 100 page portfolio which included* *write-ups, pictures and images of positive experiences throughout her career. As she worked on this project, she began to change her perception of herself and her abilities.*

Grace told me that the process of creating the portfolio illustrated to her that she was a very successful, capable and accomplished woman – the exact opposite of the woman she used to think that she was. Within three weeks from our first meeting, Grace felt so excited and confident that she booked the appointment with her boss, discussed a transition plan and accepted the promotion.

Focusing on the *positive* allowed Grace to immerse herself and her attention on her successes, which helped her to re-evaluate the old beliefs she held about herself. Over time, by contrasting her old negative thoughts with an avalanche of powerful positive thoughts, Grace gained new trust in herself, her competence and achievements, and found herself believing the positive affirmations versus the negative.

In the emerging fields of neuropsychology and Neuro-Linguistic Programming this technique is known as **reconditioning. When the old negative memories and more powerful positive experiences are held in consciousness at the same time**, the neural networks for both fire simultaneously, causing a re-wiring of the neural networks. Another life-changing benefit that stems from reliving previous accomplishments is a shift in your emotions and an elevation of your mood, which further motivates you to go after what you want.

In my practice I also use the **"collapsing the anchors" technique**, which is covered in-depth in the chapter on Formative Experiences and Anchors. This particular therapeutic method helps people to overcome triggers from their past, using techniques adapted from classical conditioning. When someone is affected by negative triggers, which could be elicited by any number of neutral stimuli such as hearing a specific phrase, being exposed to a certain person, situation or even physical reaction that stems from a negative association, they experience a cascade of out-of-control behaviours that are way more upsetting than the situation calls for.

Collapsing the anchors is a concept borrowed from Exposure therapy, where people who suffer from life-crippling anxiety and phobias get gradually immersed or exposed to the stimuli that causes their fears. Over time, this repeated exposure creates a new association where the individual feels less uncomfortable and more in control. When I work on this with clients, we add an additional step – overexposure to positive associations, stimuli and experiences, which also helps to collapse the anchors associated with old conditioned responses.

Sometimes we don't see our **limiting thoughts and beliefs** as easily as Grace did. She knew exactly what she was saying to herself that made her to feel less-than. I have found it useful to get clients to create an inventory of all the disempowering things they are saying to themselves in order to bring them into conscious awareness. One client told me that after he created his inventory, he was so shocked at how much he complained and blamed others for what's happening in his life. He wanted to work with me after attending a workshop and hearing me say something that he found transformative and applicable to his issues.

"Imagine that complaining and blaming is your mind's way of fooling you into believing that you did something about your problem. But this is disempowering and promotes a feeling of helplessness because nothing really changes. Every time you blame, you give away your power and don't believe in your own ability to help yourself."

This next exercise is one that I do with participants of my Personal Mastery Workshop, which I facilitate twice a year. I call this the '**I am too...**' **exercise**. Each person is asked to sit back and reflect on all the disempowering statements that they say to themselves or to others, which always start with "I am too...", "I can't..." or "I'm not...".

Common examples of disempowering phrases are, *'I am too old to start this,'* or *'I can't help getting angry'* or *'I'm not good enough.'*

Here's your chance to do an negative phases inventory. In column one of this chart, jot down as many phrases as you can think of that are like the examples above, and reflect on how they make you feel.

What do you say or think about yourself and / or say to others about yourself?	How does this make you feel?

Once you complete your inventory of disempowering phrases, you may want to re-evaluate which ones are limiting your progress. Notice how they typically elicit negative feelings and demotivate you from taking action.

In my book Passage To Prosperity, I describe the **Belief Replacement Method**. This is a three step method that you can use to re-program the limiting beliefs. Here's a summary of how the method works.

The first step is for you to become aware of the limiting belief and write it down. In step two, as you hear yourself saying this phrase or as it bubbles up in your mind, you need to immediately say to yourself, "Stop/Cancel-cancel, I no longer believe this about myself." The final step is to have a powerful positive affirmation/belief that you say to yourself which replaces, counteracts and neutralizes the old belief.

Use the chart below to map out this process for the limiting beliefs you would like to work on.

Belief Replacement Method Chart:

Example of limiting belief: I will never succeed.	Say: Cancel-cancel – I no longer believe this about myself.	Replacement: I have the skills and mindset to do anything I desire.

Behavioural Flexibility

Another key aspect of Personal Mastery is **behavioural flexibility**, which is your ability to shift your behaviour to better relate to and connect with others around you. This requires an understanding of your own personal preferences and biases when you communicate and interact with others. Behavioural flexibility also requires that you are able to read or perceive the needs of others in order to adapt to their style of communication and social engagement. This does not mean you don't express yourself authentically, but it does mean that your ability to listen and flex to others will create the foundation for positive interactions with those around you. Essentially, I am referring to the process of building *rapport* with people so they feel comfortable and understood by you. Once they trust and feel in sync with you, they will also reciprocate.

Rapport building is the foundation of effective communication and influence. Rapport is that feeling of being in sync with someone. When we are in Rapport with others, we feel a strong sense of connection, which in turn establishes a sense of trust. We can leverage this trust to build deeper relationships and connections with our family, friends and colleagues. We can learn a lot more about a person because they feel comfortable sharing their innermost feelings and thoughts with us.

So, how do we build Rapport?

In a nutshell, Rapport means finding ways to make the person you are talking to feel that you are similar and have things in common. *When people are alike they tend to like each other.* Therefore, when the intention is to create rapport, we should try to match the other person's body language, facial gestures, breathing pattern and the words they are using. What are they wearing? What common experiences do you share with them? Mirroring and matching any of these characteristics will help them to feel at ease with you. When they are at ease, they will be more receptive to building a strong supportive connection with you.

We build rapport by sharing common experiences, and through mirroring and matching the following:

- Body language and facial gestures
- Voice and tonality
- Language – Key words and phrases

*Imagine you are meeting someone for the first time. First, you shake hands. Then, as you both take your seats, you notice they rest their elbows on the table. To build rapport with a matching behaviour, you could place both hands on the table. This will a step toward getting in sync with each other. This fires up both of your **mirror neurons**, a special group of brain cells that are triggered when you perform a behaviour or when you observe someone else performing the same behaviour.*

Build strong social connections

Rapport building is an essential skill for developing strong social connections. We should develop and use our rapport building skills to cultivate mutually beneficial relationships with family, friends and teammates in order to create a support network. Everyone flourishes in supportive, compassionate and nurturing communities.

Dr. Steven Porges published his research findings on **Polyvagal Theory**, a groundbreaking therapeutic approach for healing trauma and helping us build healthy lives, which proposes that *"connectedness is truly a biological imperative. We are wired to connect with others and seek mutually beneficial relationships."*

Polyvagal theory studies different parts of the nervous system and how they respond in stressful situations. The various branches of the vagal nerve (the 10th cranial nerve), serve different *evolutionary stress responses*: the more primitive branch elicits *immobilization behaviors* (e.g. to freeze and pretend to be dead), whereas the more evolved branch is linked to *social communication and self-soothing behaviors*. The primitive freeze function is only active if the more evolved functions (*e.g. the mobilizing fight and flight responses*) fail to protect us. These vagus neural pathways regulate automatic responses and the expression of emotional and social behaviour.

Polyvagal Theory postulates that it is the physiological state of these neural pathways that dictate the range of behaviour and psychological experiences one possesses. This theory has many implications for the study of stress, emotion and social behaviour.

A noteworthy aspect for the purpose of understanding *the importance of social connections* is the **Social Engagement System**, *which is the most evolved branch of our nervous system. This component is active when we feel safe, secure and connected to others.* In contrast, when the primitive functions are activated, we are *disassociated*, feeling separate and cut off from others due to being in survival mode. Dissociation and zoning out really affects higher, executive brain functions, which are essential for critical thinking and decision-making.

An important intervention to help someone who has an activated primitive function is to re-engage them by instructing them to move around so they can snap out of their frozen state, and then asking them to look around and point out things they see in their surroundings. This is a tool I use when I bring someone out of hypnosis to ensure they have full awareness and are back in the present.

We are designed to seek out mutually beneficial relationships – this is an evolutionary advantage wired into our biological development. The Social Engagement System *enhances our skills for bonding, attachment and emotional intimacy.* When this system is active, we connect and communicate with those around us. This also mitigates our fear-based response system, thereby keeping us physiologically relaxed and emotionally calm. In this regulated state, we feel more resourceful and resilient.

Every Personal Mastery plan needs to include steps for building and maintaining *strong nurturing networks of supportive people.* This can start at home with family and friends. Then with your team members at work, and in the larger community. This involves taking up activities that require interacting with others, such as sports, hobbies, dance or yoga classes, community events and other prosocial behaviours.

Epigenetics and Resilience

The emerging field of **Epigenetics** provides additional evidence of the importance of nurturing in our early development. Epigenetics is the story of how *nurture* affects our *nature.* Epigenetics literally means 'above' genetics. It refers to environmental factors that create modifications to DNA that turn genes 'on' or 'off.' These modifications do not change the DNA sequence, but instead, they affect how cells "read" the genes.

A core finding of epigenetics is that trauma is inheritable and passed down through generations. The offspring of those who have survived wartime, famine, genocides, major upheaval and traumatic events are often at greater risk for developing post-traumatic stress (PTSD) and other physical ailments. For instance, the children and grandchildren of Holocaust survivors who were interned in concentration camps tended to be born smaller and predisposed to diabetes, stress and anxiety – a direct result of their ancestors' slowed metabolism and mental shock.

Epigenetic research has shown that how we react to stress is often inherited from our parents and grandparents or experiences early in life; these epigenetic tags can make a person more or less susceptible to stress and fear.

A watershed study at Emory University demonstrated how fear and stress can be transmitted intergenerationally. Male mice were conditioned to pair the scent of cherry blossoms with electric shock, and then were bred with regular mice. For 3 generations, their offspring showed intense fear and stress reactions to the smell of cherry blossoms despite never being electroshocked. The offspring were born with adapted changes already hardwired into their brains – an over-developed, better sense of smell and stronger fear receptors.

The conclusions of the Emory Study were that mice exposed to extreme stress had offspring who also experienced heightened fear response and increased stress hormone levels despite never experiencing the stressful environment their fathers and grandfathers had endured.

In another epigenetic experiment, mice were removed from their mothers early on, recreating what would be a major childhood trauma in humans. Those mice were found to have heightened fear and anxiety as adults. These traits were also passed down to the next two generations of offspring despite the fact their offspring were never separated from their mothers.

Biology doesn't know good or bad - epigenetic changes are made to fit the environment you or your predecessors are in. These changes are meant to adapt you for survival - to make you survive. They are meant to be an evolutionary advantage - whatever changes happen in the new environment, our bodies will adapt and adjust.

It's important to recognize that as organisms, our bodies are biologically built for resilience - to survive whatever comes our way. If a period of starvation is anticipated, a fetus's epigenetic tags will slow down its metabolism and keep it smaller in size, requiring less nutrition from its mother. However, while needed in the beginning, occasionally epigenetic changes no longer serve as positive. This is where epigenetic therapy comes in.

Epigenetic changes are not necessarily negative. We are wired to survive. And early research into this fascinating new field is showing that mindfulness and other cognitive therapies can help to modify and alleviate the epigenetics expression that may predispose some to anxiety, stress and other physical ailments.

Resolving conflict

Managing conflict and difficult conversations are extremely important skills for achieving Personal Mastery. The following chart illustrates a method for conflict resolution. This process can be used to resolve personal and professional situations.

Process Step	Description
What is the key issue?	
Specific behaviour	
The feelings – theirs and yours	
What is at stake?	
What is your contribution?	
What is the other person's contribution?	

Discuss both perspectives on the issue	
How will you both change (the solution)	
Implement the solution	
Evaluate how things are working	

To sum it up, Personal Mastery is all about building healthy habits and rituals that support you in creating a life of fulfilment and well-being. Personal Mastery is all about gaining a more thorough knowledge of ourselves so that we know which thoughts are disempowering and should be challenged to reduce their self-limiting effects, and which habits and thoughts are empowering and deserve to be amplified in our lives.

Learning in Action - Personal Mastery
Use the following table to plan, set timelines and track your progress on each of the components.

Component / Tools / Process	Action Plan – In the next 90 days when will you do it? Track your notes in the column below.
Building Self-Awareness – Reflection and Journaling	
Limiting Beliefs – Complete "I am too" Chart	
Belief Replacement Method – Complete 3-Step Chart	
Use **Rapport** to build support **social networks**	
Use the **Conflict Resolution process** when required	

CHAPTER NINE

Self-Identity (Bonus Chapter)

Our self-identity, also commonly known as self-concept, is our internal multi-faceted model and understanding of the 'self' as it relates to a number of characteristics such as gender, intellect, race, skills, abilities, competencies, physical characteristics and the personality we've identified for ourselves. Self-knowledge of our identities is enhanced by our self-awareness, and is impacted by our self-esteem. We are continually self-assessing ourselves and applying labels such as good, bad, lazy, and other such qualifiers.

A person's self-concept may change with time as reassessment occurs, which in extreme cases can lead to an identity crisis, or when we are confused or hurt about new revelations uncovered by what people say about us. Furthermore, self-concept is not restricted to present information; it includes past selves and future selves. Future or possible selves represent individuals' ideas of what they might become, what they would like to become, or what they are afraid of becoming. They correspond to hopes, fears, goals, and threats.

The pioneers of the study of self-concept were renowned psychologists Carl Rogers and Abraham Maslow. Rogers believed that everyone strives to become more like an "ideal self." The closer you are to your ideal self, the happier you will be. Rogers also claimed that one factor in a person's happiness is unconditional positive regard for others. Unconditional positive regard often occurs in close/familial relationships, and where we maintain a consistent level of affection regardless of the recipient's actions.

Arguments can often leave us feeling disturbed about how we appear to others. Will they think we are unstable, mean-spirited or unreasonable? Our identity is threatened if people say we are any of these things, because we don't want to believe negative things about ourselves. We want to feel worthy of love, recognition and attention; appearing as a positive and valuable person is essential to our self-image.

Unraveling our inner workings and gaining knowledge of where we have vulnerabilities in our self-identity is the best way to arm ourselves against behaving in ways that cause us to become off-balanced. If we have foreknowledge of the extreme tendencies we have inherited from our experiences, we can avoid acting in inappropriate ways.

Many of these tendencies could be considered *defense mechanisms*, which we use to protect our identities. We also need to develop an understanding of the signals we subconsciously send out through our behaviour, language and attitude, which create difficult interpersonal interactions and conversations with others. Could you be attracting contentious relationships because of unknown vulnerabilities?

You have probably encountered people whom you have to address in a particular way (i.e. handle with kid gloves) otherwise they might react explosively. They appear hypersensitive to the simplest things you may say to them. It is possible that these individuals are suffering from a mental illness such as depression; however, I have found that many individuals are driven by subconscious aspects that push them to respond in this manner. This chapter covers examples of various individuals who underwent a period of self-exploration to reveal aspects of their self-identity which they felt were detrimental to themselves and to their relationships. They wanted to shift their abrupt communication approach and release the pent-up emotions that often caused them to behave in a destructive manner.

I recently worked with a client who came to me to deal with his pattern of attracting women who, according to him, played hard to get. Whenever he became interested in someone, she turned out to be inaccessible or just rejected him. Worse, he'd had a difficult childhood where his mother was detached and rarely expressed her love.

I have seen this pattern emerge in other clients who keep trying to capture the love of the person who is a representation of the parent they most wanted to receive love from – the parent who they feel abandoned or rejected them. In this client's case, this situation manifested in the form of the unattainable women he met in his life.

He constantly repeated the pattern of trying to win their love, only to end up with more heartbreak. Essentially, his subconscious believed that if he could get these women to love him, he was metaphorically replacing the love of the parent who rejected him. His attachment to his self-identity as the nice guy was not helping him to connect with others who could appreciate him. The women he dated primarily took advantage of him. Yet, due to his low self-esteem and a desire to please, he believed that he would eventually convince them to stay with him.

His pattern defines a situation of many who have experienced rejection by a parent in childhood. We idolize an absent or neglectful parent because the child had to hold onto a belief that his parent has to love him in some way. But the obsession to recapture this love translates into an unreciprocated attraction to individuals who represent the idolized parent.

The alternative might be to reject this parent by not wanting to be like them. As such, we reject their qualities within ourselves. We judge and reject people who represent the characteristics of the neglectful parent, and we do so by developing a push-pull within ourselves – instead of integrating these aspects (our shadow selves) by accepting that we too have the capacity to be like those we idolize or reject.

When we accept our shadow selves, we take charge of the forces that drive us toward the type of people who are symbolized by the past, individuals whom we can never truly win because the whole fantasy is built upon an illusion.

Another example comes from a female client who found that she was attracted to men who were emotionally shallow, womanizing and uncaring like her own father, who had walked out on the family for another woman when my client was 15 years old.

She wanted to know how she could be attracted to someone so similar to the father who had created so much pain for her family. Why was she drawn to uncaring men who would just use and reject her? While she was acting out this pattern, she actually did not realize that she pursued men who were similar to her father. She failed to see how her subconscious expectation was that if she could win their love, it would be just like gaining the love she'd always wanted from her dad.

In our sessions, she judged and criticized her father harshly for being disloyal and abandoning the family. She was even more confused when she realized that she was tempted to act in ways which were similar to her father's behaviours. Over and over again, she acted out a "rejection signature" by behaving in a cycling pattern – either unfairly rejecting people in her life or allowing herself to be rejected by choosing to be with people who were never able to commit. She also found herself critical of her spouse and was constantly attracted to other, archetypal men who personified her father's characteristics.

Could she accept the fact that she was capable of the same actions as her father? Could she too become disloyal to her spouse? The way she was finally able to navigate through this addiction was by accepting that indeed, she did have the capacity to be just like her dad. Her lifelong rejection of him was also a rejection of aspects of herself. Now that the subconscious motivations were out in the open, they would no longer drive her actions without her cognizant awareness.

I asked her to consider that these rejected aspects of herself could be seen as her shadow self. She needed to examine this shadow and to accept the truth that would be revealed, even if negative feelings of shame and embarrassments might emerge.

EXERCISE: Figuring Out Your Shadow Self

Make a list of people you feel highly critical of. List all the characteristics that push your buttons, and then answer the following questions:

What are the characteristics you are judging or criticizing about this person?

If you had that behaviour yourself, how would it make you feel? Why do you think you would reject it in yourself?

Reflect on past actions where you have put yourself down. What negative things did the little voice at the back of your head tell you about yourself?

As you work toward unlocking a greater understanding of yourself, you become a better judge of character, which will come in handy when you attempt to read and persuade other people's motivations. Seriously examine the possibility that whatever qualities you reject in others may be a reflection of what you fear most about yourself. You need to be open to looking at all aspects of 'self' in order to see things as they really are, rather than be affected by wishful thinking.

Naturally, acceptance does not mean expression. Acknowledging that you share similar qualities with someone you dislike does not imply that these qualities will manifest the same way in you. You are a unique individual. As you go through life, you attract experiences that help you explore the things you reject within yourself. As you resist, reject, judge or criticize any attribute in someone else, it is possible that you might become more attracted to it subconsciously, and/or manifest it through destructive behaviours of your own.

When we repress whatever we cannot accept about ourselves, we build an internal void. This surfaces as hurtful behaviour towards others, such as angry outbursts that destroy healthy communication.

One client told me that she found herself addicted to "sad stuff." When I asked her what she meant, she said that she would start to imagine how her young cousins would feel if their father left them, and how they would end up with "messed-up lives". She reflected on how everyone would then understand her and why she had had a difficult life because her father left. Her little visualizations eventually led her to feel guilty and sad about wishing a negative consequence on someone else just so that she could prove a point.

In fact, she was creating scenarios where she disassociated and could **re-witness** these painful events without feeling the intensity of her own feelings. In the end she still experienced a dose of sadness; it was as if within these small doses of sadness she was slowly re-experiencing the great sadness of losing her father. Each visualization helped her witness the pain from an outsider's perspective. This is a process known in psychology as *disassociation*.

Disassociation is a powerful technique for helping us to re-evaluate and **reframe** the events in our life by viewing them from different perspectives. Often in disassociation we project onto others the feelings that reside within ourselves but we cannot confront or accept.

In psychological **projection**, we deny our own feelings and subconscious characteristics but assign them to someone else. Projection reduces negative feelings by allowing the expression of the unwanted unconscious impulses without letting the conscious mind recognize them. One type of defensive behaviour that can be considered psychological projection is *blaming*.

Blaming others is one of the primary defense mechanisms frequently used during confrontation. We are more comfortable trying to figure out what the other person did wrong, rather than looking at their own contribution. We want to avoid the discomfort of owing up to our faults, so it is easier to blame the other person for creating the disagreement. In essence, we project faults onto those around us and remain unconscious of our own weaknesses.

We may find ourselves testing people who are closest to us. This is a common tendency: *"Let's see how much of our crap they will take before they reject us; if they keep putting up with it, they must really love us."*

We self-sabotage our opportunity for happiness by pushing away our loved ones with these tests. The natural consequence is we begin to feel guilty for hurting our family and friends. It is a form of self-punishment where, as we ill-treat those around us, they react with self-protection or defensiveness and in turn reject us. The more we act out this relationship pattern, the more it becomes reinforced until it becomes a habit, automatically being triggered by the most inane circumstances.

We develop an unending cycle of inflicting pain and feeling guilt. To deal with it, we create justifications for why we behaved the way we did, get angry again and finally re-inflict the pain. We are trapped, hostage to repeating the same cycle again and again. I call this the **cycle of revenge**, because we feel justified in exacting retribution for all the wrongs we perceive to have experienced.

As you're reading the examples in this chapter, you might recognize similar patterns in yourself or others. You might also be wondering if people can really change parts of their self-identity in any real permanent way. The answer is *Yes*, people can and do change. It starts with a burning desire to have more harmonious relations with others.

Awareness is the first step toward meaningful change. Then you must choose to change. Choose to forgive or apologize. Choose to let go. Then take action. Do the exercises outlined in this chapter and throughout the book. You will soon begin to break unhealthy habits, thereby reducing the effects of the guilt, frustration or the anger 'button' being pushed.

Taking charge in this way means having a great deal less conflict in your life. This is your reward for exploring aspects of your self-identity and reconciling underlying triggers that cause you to behave in non-constructive ways.

Final words

Having come to the end of this book, you are now ready to put your learning in action. You have access to powerful tools at your disposal – meditation scripts to retrain your awareness, visualization exercises, how-to tools and questionnaires to optimize your mind for greater self-regulation, reduced stress and increased performance.

In an ever-changing world where resilience and emotional intelligence are key to achieving success and happiness, developing personal mastery is crucial to overcoming obstacles and living your best life.

APPENDIX I

Glossary

Amygdala – Deep within our brain's temporal lobe there is an almond-shaped mass of nuclei called the amygdala. This part of the brain plays a primary role in the processing and storage of our emotional reactions. When we feel fear, the fear stimuli is processed by the amygdala, where they are associated with memories of the stimuli and a fear response is elicited.

Anchors are stimuli-response pairings that can be triggered intentionally or accidentally.

Automaticity is the ability to do things without occupying the mind because the behaviour has become a habit, an automatic response pattern. Automaticity is a form of deep subconscious learning (called subconscious competence) due to the repetition, reinforcement and practice of a specific behaviour or thought.

Attention bias is when you pay attention to certain details more so than others due to what you value or believe. This is potentially what is happening in an argument, where we are predisposed to pay attention to what we expect to hear.

Behavioural flexibility is defined as the ability to shift our behaviour and communication style based upon the situation and the person with whom we are communicating. Behavioural flexibility is possible if we first understand ourselves and simultaneously have a process for reading others.

Cognitive bias is the tendency to process and filter information through our own experiences, likes and dislikes; it is especially prevalent during arguments. We become more and more incapable to accurately process what the other person is trying to make us understand.

Cognitive Dissonance is the tension produced by holding two competing or conflicting thoughts in our minds at the same time.

Defensiveness is characterized by being off-balanced, flustered and under emotional hijack.

Disassociation is a powerful technique for helping us to re-evaluate and **reframe** the events in our life by viewing them from different perspectives.

Emotional Hijack is a word used to describe the fear reaction which hijacks our higher thinking, leading us to interpret the situation in ways that dramatically skew our perception of reality. Our emotions grow out of control and we become hypersensitive to what is happening around us.

Emotional intelligence (EI) can be defined as the ability, skill, and self-perceived ability to identify, assess, and control the emotions of oneself and others.

Emotional literacy is defined as the ability to understand your emotions, the ability to listen to others and empathize with their emotions, and the ability to express emotions productively.

Escalation of commitment is the tendency to put in more and more resources in an obvious losing proposition due to the time, effort, emotions and money that you have already invested.

Empathetic listening is a way of listening and responding to the client that enhances mutual understanding.

Interrupt the pattern is a way to change behaviour in order to break the cycle of a ritual.

Ideomotor effect is a term that refers to the automatic muscular reflex response that occurs due to a thought. Under hypnosis I may prompt a client to indicate a "yes" or "no" response with a specific finger, or even to raise a hand if they feel any discomfort.

Micro-behaviours refer to the breaking down and describing of small changes in a person's actions, such as shifting their posture, turning their head, yawning unexpectedly, sighing, and rolling their eyes.

Microexpressions are involuntary facial expressions which appear based upon the emotional state of the person.

Mirror neurons are a special class of brain cells that fire not only when an individual performs an action, but also when the individual observes someone else make the same movement.

Neuro-Linguistic Programming (NLP) is a term coined to describe the foundational belief of the model that there are connections between the neurological and linguistic processes which form specific behavioural patterns that have been programmed in us based upon our life experiences.

Perception is the process in which we interpret and organize stimuli to understand and give meaning to the experiences we are having.

Psychological projection is when we deny our own feelings and subconscious characteristics but assign them to someone else. Projection reduces negative feelings by allowing the expression of the unwanted unconscious impulses without letting the conscious mind recognize them.

Rapport is the feeling of being in *sync* with each other.

Reframing expands your potential by giving you another way to think, feel, do and ultimately choose how you will respond to an experience. New perspectives will create new possibilities.

Representational system defines how our minds process information through the use of our senses.

Reticular Activating System, also known as the RAS. The reticular activating system helps mediate transitions from

145

relaxed wakefulness to periods of high attention. The RAS is made up of billions of nerve cells that are densely packed at the central part of the brainstem. Another way to look at is that when you create an intention in your conscious mind you activate the RAS which heightens your awareness on a subconscious level, thereby helping you to notice more of what you want while diffusing other stimuli that you don't want. The RAS spares you from having to process all the background "noise" by screening out irrelevant data.

Selective perception is where we selectively interpret the behaviour of others based upon our particular interests, experiences and background.

Self-identity, also called self-concept, is our internal multi-faceted model and understanding of the 'self' as it relates to a number of characteristics such as gender, intellect, race, skills, abilities, competencies, physical characteristics and the personality we've identified for ourselves.

Self-fulfilling prophecy is a term used to describe the phenomenon where an individual works toward the validation of what they perceive, expect or believe.

Therapeutic Rapport is created through the active demonstration of empathy and understanding by the coach, where the client then feels a sense of safety, trust and respect.

Values are important and enduring beliefs or ideals shared by the members of a culture or family about what is good or desirable and what is not. Values exert major influence on the behavior of an individual and serve as broad guidelines in all situations.

Visualization is a mental technique that builds mental imagery to which your emotions and body responds. It will allow you to sit on your sofa and literally sense the situation as if it were real.

APPENDIX II

Bibliography

Amen, Daniel. 1998. *Change Your Brain, Change Your Life.*
New York: Three Rivers Press.

Arbinger Institute, The. 2002. *Leadership and Self-Deception.*
Barrett-Koehler San Francisco: Puslishers, Inc.

Bolton, Robert and Dorothy Grover Bolton. 2009. *People Styles at Work and Beyond, 2nd ed.* New York: Amacon.

Bonnstetter, Bill. 1993. *The Universal Language Disc.* Scottsdale: TTI, Ltd.

Burns, David D. 2000. *Feeling Good. The New Mood Therapy.* New York: Quill.

Carnegie, Dale. 1936. *How to Win Friends and Influence People.* New York: Simon & Schuster.

Cialdini, Robert. 2007. *Influence: the Psychology of Persuasion, revised edition.* New York: Harper Collins.

Dimitrius, Jo-Ellan.1999. *Reading People.* New York: Ballantine Books.

Ferryman, Claudia. 2011. *The Communication Chameleon.* Toronto: Rainmaker Books.

Forward, Susan. 1997. *Emotional Blackmail.* New York: HarperCollins Publisher.

Gerstner Jr., Louis V. 2002. Who Says Elephants Can't Dance?
New York: HarperCollins Publishers, Inc.

Goleman, Daniel. 2002. *Primal Leadership*. Boston: Havard Business School Press.

Goleman, Daniel. 1998. *Emotional Intelligence*. New York: Bantam Press.

Kouzes, James M. and Barry Z. Posner. 2002. *Leadership Challenge, 3rd ed*. San Francisco: Jossey-Bass.

Langton, Nancy and Stephen P. Robbins. 2007. *Organizational Behaviour Canadian 4th ed*. Toronto: Pearson-Prentice Hall.

Latham, Gary P. 2009. *Becoming the Evidence-Based Manager*. Boston: Davies-Black

Levine, Peter A. 1997. *Walking the Tiger*. Berkeley: North Atlantic Books

Mehrabian, Albert. 1971. *Implicit Communication of Emotions and Attitudes,* 2nd ed. Belmont, CA: Wadsworth.

Murray, Joseph.2008. *The Power of Your Subconscious Mind*. New York: Prentice Hall Press

Porges, Stephen. 2017. *Accessing the Healing Power of the Vagus Nerve*. Berkeley: North Atlantic Books

Posen, David. 2013. *Is Work Killing You?*. Canada: House of Anansi Press Inc.

Rotman Magazine. Fall 2010. *It's Complicated*. Toronto: University of Toronto. Rotman Magazine. Winter 2011. *Thinking About Thinking II*. Toronto: University of Toronto.

Stone, Douglas, Bruce Patton, Sheila Heen. 2010. *Difficult Conversations, 10th anniversary edition*. New York: Penguin.

Van der Kolk, Bessel. 2014.*The Body Keeps The Score-Brain, Mind & Body in Healing Trauma*. New York: Penguin Books.

RECOMMENDED RESOURCES

Keynote Speaking Engagements

Claudia Ferryman is a highly sought-after keynote speaker. Her message conveys the perfect blend of conceptual and practical strategies. Claudia utilizes passion and humour to engage the audience. She has been a keynote guest speaker for numerous corporations and not-for-profit organizations. Participants are known to leave workshops saying *"That was the best presentation I've ever attended!"*

Dynamic Communications

Dynamic Communication is a behaviorally-based communication seminar aimed at teaching people how to communicate using specialized techniques and methods to understand themselves and others. The seminar incorporates a behavioral assessment to give a more complete understanding of each individual. Participants learn how to interact with others and to appreciate each others' behavioral styles. Improved communication is noticed immediately after the seminar. *This workshop is certified for continuing educational credits.* The training is based upon the DISC Communication Model.

Leadership Development Program

This leadership program is made up of 12 workshops that cover subjects such as leadership styles, communication, conflict resolution, psychology of influence, decision-making, strategic planning, change management and more. Each participant will complete an online validated *Leadership Assessment* that outlines their core competencies, emotional intelligence, communication preferences and motivational factors. This program can be completed as integrated 12 modules or select stand-alone workshops.

Team Building

This workshop is designed to enhance *team effectiveness*. You will be exposed to practical methodologies used to develop cohesive teams who communicate and work together in a more effective and productive manner. You will gain access to the most advanced, leading-edge skills for mobilizing cross-functional teams. Learn the reasons why teams fail and how to motivate individuals to work collaboratively by understanding the fundamental characteristics, communication styles and motivations of one another.

Powerful Speaking and Presenting Skills

This course is designed for anyone who has to facilitate meetings, train or present to groups of people. Participants will discover the underlying factors that affect how individuals learn and what motivates them. You will gain knowledge about communication techniques, learning strategies, special listening skills and how to capture and maintain the attention of your audience. Training includes experiential exercises, lectures, demonstration and self-assessment surveys.

Assessment Profiles

Assessment profiles are available for communication styles, leadership preferences, sales / job competencies, relationship styles, emotional intelligence and motivation factors.

To reserve Claudia Ferryman or book one of these workshops for your next event, email info@rainmakerstrategies.org or call 1-416-410-1614.

ABOUT THE AUTHOR

Claudia Ferryman is a renowned keynote speaker and sought-after consultant with more than 20 years of experience and expertise in organizational psychology, communication, influence & persuasion, and leadership development. She is CEO of Rainmaker Strategies Group and an instructor at the University of Toronto, where she has received the Award of Excellence in Teaching.

Claudia has worked with corporations such as Rogers, Motorola, Kodak, Bell, Rotman School of Management, CIBC, Moneris Solutions (Bank of Montreal/Royal Bank joint venture), as well as government ministries, boards of education and multiple non-profit and community service groups to solve difficult organizational problems by guiding them on what has been described as an engaging, fast-paced and experiential journey inside the deeper psychological motivations that drive behaviour.

Claudia enjoys taking complex concepts and presenting them in ways that are easy to understand and apply. She has improved the performance and productivity of numerous teams by imparting powerful techniques on how to get better results through leveraging communication in a wide range of professional contexts. She holds a degree in organizational psychology and multiple certifications in Leadership, Emotional Intelligence, Mindfulness, Compassion Fatigue, NLP and behavioural/values analysis.

Made in the USA
Middletown, DE
27 June 2021